The Cupcake

The Cupcake

Life's better with
a cupcake

First published in 2011
LOVE FOOD is an imprint of Parragon Books Ltd

Parragon
Chartist House
15-17 Trim Street
Bath BA1 1HA, UK
www.parragon.com

ISBN: 978-1-4454-3806-1

Printed in China

Introduction and new recipes by Angela Drake
Cover and internal photography by Clive Streeter
Home economy by Angela Drake and Teresa Goldfinch

Notes for the Reader
This book uses both metric and imperial measurements. Follow the same units of measurement throughout; do not mix metric and imperial. All spoon measurements are level: teaspoons are assumed to be 5 ml, and tablespoons are assumed to be 15 ml. Unless otherwise stated, milk is assumed to be full fat, eggs and individual vegetables are medium, and pepper is freshly ground black pepper.

The times given are an approximate guide only. Preparation times differ according to the techniques used by different people and the cooking times may also vary from those given. Optional ingredients, variations or serving suggestions have not been included in the calculations.

Recipes using raw or very lightly cooked eggs should be avoided by infants, the elderly, pregnant women, convalescents and anyone suffering from an illness. Pregnant and breastfeeding women are advised to avoid eating peanuts and peanut products. Sufferers from nut allergies should be aware that some of the ready-made ingredients used in the recipes in this book may contain nuts. Always check the packaging before use.

Introduction

Who can resist the sweet and delicious charms of a cupcake? Easy to make, simple to decorate and perfect for any occasion, the cupcake has become everyone's favourite cake!

From tiny bite-sized mini cupcakes or the delicately iced English fairy cakes to fabulously over-the-top frosted cakes or fun novelty cakes, cupcakes are incredibly versatile creations. Conveniently packaged in their own paper cases, they are certainly the simplest of all cakes to make but, once decorated, they can become the star attraction for any celebration, from a children's birthday party to a wedding.

Cupcake making is a joy for anyone, from the novice baker to the experienced cook, and for young children it's often their first experience of home baking – helping Mum to make a batch of cupcakes and then eagerly tasting the slightly wonky results!

This book has absolutely everything you need to know about making and decorating cupcakes. It has a comprehensive introduction to cupcake making, including all the basic equipment and ingredients you will need through to clear and descriptive steps for baking and frosting, as well as plenty of tips and ideas for fun and fancy decorations and perfect ways to display cupcakes or to give them as gifts.

Once you've mastered the basics, you can turn the pages and choose from any one of 80 divine cupcake recipes. From simple-to-make classic cupcakes to cute novelty designs, truly indulgent chocolate creations or elegantly decorated show-stoppers, you really will be spoilt for choice. Welcome to the wonderful world of the cupcake!

Baking Equipment

The beauty of baking cupcakes is that you really don't need a lot of expensive or fancy equipment. Most of you will have the few necessary basics in your kitchen already. Here's a list of what you'll need to get started.

Scales

Accurate measuring of ingredients is a major key to all successful baking so a good-quality set of scales is essential. Digital scales are the most accurate and some have a useful add-on facility that allows you to re-set the display to zero and weigh out another ingredient on top. Cheaper spring or balance scales are just as good if used correctly. It's essential to always follow either metric or imperial measurements for a recipe – not a mixture of both. If you use digital scales, keep a spare battery handy.

Measuring spoons

Using a set of standard measuring spoons will ensure that small quantities of ingredients, such as baking powder, bicarbonate of soda and vanilla extract, are measured accurately. They are usually sold in sets of 4, 5 or 6 spoons and will measure out between $1/4$ teaspoon and 1 tablespoon. Always use a level spoonful, unless stated otherwise in the recipe.

Mixing bowls

Although you only need a large mixing bowl for making most cupcakes, it's useful to have a selection of 2 or 3 different-sized bowls. Toughened and heatproof glass bowls are hard-wearing and practical. Melamine or ceramic bowls are available in a variety of colours and look attractive in the kitchen!

Sieves

To sift dry ingredients and remove any lumps, you will need a large metal or plastic sieve with medium to fine mesh. A small sieve is also handy for decorating cupcakes with a dusting of cocoa or icing sugar. After washing metal sieves, make sure they are thoroughly dry before putting away.

Baking Equipment

Spoons

You'll need wooden spoons for creaming and mixing, and a metal spoon for folding in ingredients. Wooden spoons are cheap to buy so it's worth having a few in a range of sizes. Always make sure they are dried thoroughly after washing and throw away any that are old or split. A good-sized metal spoon is essential for the folding-in stage of cupcake making.

Electric mixer

Although not essential, an electric mixer makes light work of cupcake making, especially if you use the all-in-one method. Chose one with at least 3 variable speed settings to prevent over-beating the mixture.

Spatulas

A flexible rubber or silicone spatula is useful for light mixing of ingredients and scraping down the mixture from the sides of bowls. A spatula with a spoon-shaped tip is ideal for scooping up mixture to fill piping bags.

Bun/muffin trays

To ensure even cooking and a good shape, cupcakes are best baked in metal or silicone bun or muffin trays. They usually have 6 or 12 holes to sit paper cases in. Some metal trays have a non-stick coating, which is useful if you want to make cupcakes without paper cases. Flexible silicone trays come in a variety of bright colours and can also be used without paper cases.

Bun trays usually have fairly shallow holes with gently sloping sides whereas muffin trays have much deeper holes with straighter sides. The type of tray you use will affect the appearance of your cupcakes – for a slightly flatter and wider cupcake use a bun tray, and for deep cupcakes with straight sides use a muffin tray. To make mini cupcakes, you'll need a mini muffin tray.

Wire cooling rack

Once baked, cupcakes need to be transferred to a wire cooling rack to allow them to cool quickly and evenly. If you plan to make batches of cupcakes, it would be useful to invest in a tiered wire rack, which will save on worktop space.

Decorating Equipment

Baking cases

You'll find a huge range of paper baking cases available in shops and online. As a general guide, there are 4 different sizes of cases.

♡ **Muffin cases** – large deep cases with straight sides, these are perfect for making big American-style cupcakes.

♡ **Medium-sized cases** – these are similar in size to muffin cases, but tend to have narrower bases and hold a little less mixture.

♡ **Fairy cake/bun cases** – shallow cases that produce small English-style fairy cakes.

♡ **Mini muffin cases** – ideal for bite-sized mini cupcakes.

Silicone cases are a fantastic modern invention and are available in a range of colours, sizes and novelty designs. Most stand up by themselves so you won't need a muffin or bun tray – just pop them on a baking sheet. The main advantage of using these is that they are reusable.

In every recipe in this book, you can use any size of case but remember not to over-fill them and adjust the cooking time accordingly.

Piping bags and nozzles

For piping big swirls of cream or buttercream on top of cupcakes, choose either a large reusable plastic piping bag or disposable plastic piping bags. Both can be fitted with large star or plain nozzles.

For more intricate decorations, invest in a piping kit that contains a small plastic-lined cloth piping bag, a number of small metal piping nozzles and a coupler that allows you to change nozzles without emptying the bag. Alternatively, buy a pack of small silicone paper piping bags or make your own from greaseproof paper (see page 31).

Cutters

Round plain or fluted cutters are ideal for stamping out rounds of sugar paste to top cupcakes. Small shaped cutters (hearts, numbers, flowers etc) are great for simple but effective decorations.

Rolling pin

For rolling out small quantities of marzipan or sugar paste, it's worth buying a small non-stick rolling pin from a specialist cake decorating shop.

Palette knives

To swirl frosting onto cupcakes, you'll need a medium-sized palette knife. A small angled palette knife is also useful for lifting and placing sugar paste shapes or other decorations onto the top of cupcakes.

Food colourings

Food colourings are available in a variety of colours in either in paste or liquid form. Pastes give a good deep colour and are best for colouring marzipan, fondant icing and royal icing. Liquid colourings can be used for colouring glacé icing and buttercream.

Fun with shapes !

Ingredients

Butter or margarine

Lightly salted butter or soft tub margarine can be used to make cupcakes, although butter will give a richer and creamier flavour. Whichever you choose, remove it from the refrigerator at least 1 hour before starting to bake as it needs to be soft all the way through to be successfully creamed with the sugar. For the best flavour, use unsalted butter for buttercream.

Sugar

Caster sugar has fine grains, which make it ideal to cream smoothly with butter or margarine. Other sugars, such as soft brown or muscovado, will give a darker sponge with a richer caramel flavour. Icing sugar has a fine powdery texture and dissolves easily – perfect for buttercream and royal and glacé icings.

Flour

Most cupcake recipes use self-raising flour, although some may use plain flour with the addition of baking powder or bicarbonate of soda. Always check that self-raising flour has not passed its best before date as the raising agent will be less effective. To incorporate as much air and lightness into the cupcake mixture as possible, sift the flour before using. If using wholemeal flour, remember to tip any bran left in the sieve into the mixing bowl as this is the most nutritious and flavoursome part.

Eggs

For the best baking results, always use fresh eggs at room temperature. If eggs are too cold, they will curdle the creamed butter and sugar mixture. Be sure to use the correct egg size for the recipe – all the recipes in this book use medium eggs, unless stated otherwise.

Raising agents

Both baking powder and bicarbonate of soda are used as raising agents to produce light and airy cupcakes. Only buy in small quantities and check the best before date before using.

Flavouring extracts

Vanilla and almond extracts – when used sparingly – can add a wealth of flavour to a simple cupcake mixture, and other natural extracts, such as lemon, orange and peppermint, are also available. For delicately scented cupcakes, invest in a small bottle of rose or orange flower water.

Top Tips for Success

♡ Always preheat the oven before you start baking. As all ovens are different, use the temperature in the recipe as a guide. If your oven runs a little hot or cold then adjust the temperature accordingly. An oven thermometer is useful, especially if you have an older oven that doesn't have a light indicating when the required temperature is reached. Fan ovens tend to be hotter than conventional ovens, so reduce the temperature by 10–20 degrees or follow the manufacturer's recommendations.

♡ Assemble all the ingredients and make sure that you have enough of each ingredient – you don't want to have to dash out for another egg halfway through the recipe! Butter or margarine and eggs should be at room temperature. The butter should be of a soft, spreadable consistency.

♡ Make sure that all ingredients are carefully weighed. Too much or too little of any one ingredient and you will have less than perfect results.

♡ Cream the butter and sugar thoroughly until the mixture is very pale and fluffy. This will take at least 5 minutes by hand or 3–4 minutes with an electric mixer.

♡ Add the beaten eggs to the creamed mixture about 1 tablespoonful at a time. Beat thoroughly after each addition to make sure all the egg has been incorporated before adding the next spoonful. If you add the egg too quickly, the mixture will start to curdle. If the creamed mixture does start to curdle, stir in a spoonful of the weighed flour before adding more egg.

♡ Don't over-mix when folding in the flour otherwise you'll knock out all the air you've just whisked in! Use a light cutting and folding action and make sure to scoop up all the mixture from the bottom of the bowl.

♡ If you follow the all-in-one method, the recipe will call for a little extra raising agent to compensate for the air not being incorporated during the initial creaming stage. You'll need to use an electric mixer for this method and take care only to beat enough to combine all the ingredients to a smooth and creamy mixture.

♡ When spooning the mixture into the paper cases, take care not to overfill them. They should be about two-thirds full. Use a dessert spoon and slide the mixture off the spoon into each case with your little finger or another spoon. To fill mini muffin cases, use a teaspoon.

♡ Once the cakes are in the oven, don't be tempted to take a peek too soon. Opening the oven door will allow cold air to rush in, which will make the cakes sink in the middle.

♡ To check if the cakes are ready, press the tops gently with your fingertip – the sponge should feel just firm and spring back without leaving an indentation.

♡ Once baked, leave the cupcakes in the bun or muffin trays for 5–10 minutes to allow them to firm up a little. If you try to move them too quickly, they will crumble. Allow the cupcakes to cool completely before icing or decorating.

♡ It almost goes without saying that a cupcake is best eaten on the day of making. However, you can store undecorated cupcakes in an airtight box for 2–3 days. Depending on the topping, decorated cupcakes will keep for 1–2 days in an airtight box. It's best not to store cupcakes in the refrigerator unless they have a chocolate or cream-based topping. Remove from the refrigerator at least 30 minutes before serving. Plain and buttercream-iced cupcakes can be frozen for up to 1 month.

What went wrong?

Over peaked – too much raising agent or oven temperature too hot.

Dip in the centre – not cooked for long enough and/or oven door opened too soon.

Dense and heavy texture – insufficient creaming or too heavy handed when folding in.

Basic Vanilla Cupcakes

Follow these 10 simple steps for success every time.

MAKES 12

115 g/4 oz butter, softened, or soft margarine

115 g/4 oz caster sugar

2 eggs, lightly beaten

1 tsp vanilla extract

115 g/4 oz self-raising flour

1 tbsp milk

Step 1

Preheat the oven to 180°C/350°F/Gas Mark 4. Put 12 paper cases in a bun tray.

Step 2

Put the butter and caster sugar in a large bowl. Using a wooden spoon or an electric mixer, beat together until the mixture is pale, light and fluffy.

Step 3

Gradually beat in the eggs. Add about 1 tablespoonful at a time and beat thoroughly after each addition.

Step 4

Beat in the vanilla extract. Using a large metal sieve, sift the flour into the bowl.

Step 5

Using a metal spoon, gently fold the flour into the mixture until thoroughly incorporated.

Step 6

Add the milk and fold gently into the mixture.

Step 7

The cupcake mixture should have a smooth consistency and drop easily from the spoon if tapped on the side of the bowl.

Step 8

Carefully spoon the mixture into the paper cases, taking care not to over-fill them.

Step 9

Bake in the preheated oven for 15–20 minutes, until the cupcakes are risen, golden and just firm to the touch.

Step 10

Leave the cupcakes in the tray for about 10 minutes, then carefully transfer to a wire cooling rack. Leave to cool completely.

Flavour variations

Lemon or orange – add the finely grated rind of 1 small lemon or orange to the butter and sugar in step 2.

Chocolate – replace 2 tablespoons of the self-raising flour with cocoa powder.

Coffee – replace the milk with 1 tablespoon of cold strong black coffee.

Almond – replace the vanilla extract with 1 teaspoon of almond extract.

Peppermint – replace the vanilla extract with 1 teaspoon of peppermint extract.

Vanilla Buttercream

Smooth and buttery, vanilla-flavoured buttercream frosting is the ideal topping for cupcakes. It's simple to make, keeps well, is easy to spread or pipe and tastes delicious!

TOPS 12 CUPCAKES

150 g/5½ oz unsalted butter, softened

1 tsp vanilla extract

280 g/10 oz icing sugar

1–2 tbsp milk

Step 1

Place the butter and vanilla extract in a large mixing bowl and, using an electric mixer, beat the butter until very soft and pale.

Step 2

Gradually sift in the icing sugar, beating well after each addition. The more you beat at this stage, the lighter and fluffier the frosting will be. Beat in the milk to give a softer consistency for piping.

☆ If not using straightaway, transfer the buttercream to a small bowl and cover with clingfilm. It will keep in a cool place for 2–3 days. Stored in the refrigerator, buttercream will keep for up to a week but will become very firm, so leave at room temperature for at least 1 hour before using.

☆ To colour, use a cocktail stick to add a tiny amount of food colouring paste or liquid to the buttercream. Beat thoroughly until you have an even colour.

Flavour variations

Chocolate – beat in 2 tablespoons of cocoa powder mixed to a paste with a little hot water, or 115 g/4 oz melted milk or plain chocolate.

Lemon or orange – beat in the finely grated rind and juice of 1 large lemon or orange and omit the milk.

Coffee – replace the milk with 1–2 tablespoons of cold strong black of coffee or 1 tablespoon coffee and chicory essence.

Caramel – beat in 1–2 tablespoons of dulce de leche (caramel sauce).

Frosting Cupcakes By Hand

The simplest way to top cupcakes with buttercream is to spread or swirl the frosting with a palette knife. Here's a quick guide to a variety of different finishes.

First, make sure that the buttercream is as smooth and creamy as possible with no small lumps by beating thoroughly with a spatula.

For a simple lightly swirled topping, take a good scoop of buttercream on the palette knife and place it on the top of the cupcake. Spread the frosting to the edges of the cupcake and, using a to-and-fro motion and without lifting the palette knife from the frosting, spread the buttercream evenly over the cake.

To create a smooth domed effect, perfect for coating with sugar sprinkles, add more buttercream to the centre of the cupcake. Use the palette knife to smooth the frosting right down to the edge of the cupcake case, then lightly smooth the top.

To achieve a raised edge effect, add a little more buttercream and spread it out to the edges of the cupcake leaving a small dip in the middle. Holding the palette knife at an angle to the side of the cupcake, drag it all around the cupcake to give smooth raised edge of frosting.

For a really generously topped cupcake with big swirls of frosting, add another scoop of buttercream to the top of the cupcake. Drag the end of the knife through the frosting in the centre of the cupcake in a circular motion to create a deep swirl. Without lifting the knife from the frosting, drag it back in the opposite direction, then quickly lift the knife away.

Piping Buttercream

Piping buttercream onto cupcakes gives a professional finish and is surprisingly easy.

♡ **To fill a piping bag with frosting**, use a large piping bag fitted with a star or plain nozzle. Hold the piping bag in 1 hand with the top of the bag folded down over your fingers and thumb. Use a spatula to scoop the frosting into the bag. Unfold the top of the bag, then gently smooth the frosting down into the bag to remove any pockets of air. Twist the bag tightly at the top to prevent the frosting from being squeezed up and out of the bag.

Alternatively, you can place the piping bag in a tall glass and fold the top of the bag over the rim of the glass. This will leave you with both hands free to fill the bag with frosting.

♡ **To pipe swirls of frosting**, use a piping bag fitted with a large star nozzle and position the tip of the piping nozzle near the outer edge of the top of the cupcake. Squeeze the piping bag firmly and, as the frosting comes out of the nozzle, gently rotate the piping bag in a decreasing circle towards the centre of the cake. Once the top of the cupcake is covered, stop squeezing the bag and lift the nozzle gently away from the cupcake to give a pointed peak of frosting in the centre.

♡ **For large swirls of frosting**, pipe 2 or 3 decreasing circles of frosting on top of the cupcake, gently lifting the bag as you go.

♡ **To pipe rose swirls of frosting**, use a medium-sized star nozzle and start piping from the centre of the cupcake. Keep the nozzle close to the top of the cupcake and continue piping in a spiral pattern until the cake is covered.

Filling a piping bag

Ready to pipe

Swirls of frosting

Rose swirls

Glacé Icing

Glacé icing is simply made from icing sugar and water. It gives a lovely smooth finish to cupcakes and sets softly in about 30 minutes. It's easy to flavour and colour and can be used to create pretty feathering or fanning effects or can be simply drizzled over cupcakes.

TOPS 12 CUPCAKES

175 g/6 oz icing sugar

5–6 tsp warm water

Step 1

Sift the icing sugar into a bowl. Add 2 teaspoons of the warm water and beat well with a wooden spoon.

Step 2

Continue adding the water a little at a time until you have a smooth and thick icing that will coat the back of the wooden spoon.

☆Use immediately or cover the surface of the icing with clingfilm and use within 1 hour. Stir thoroughly before using and, if the icing has thickened a little, beat in a few drops of hot water.

☆To colour glacé icing, add a few drops of liquid food colouring or a very tiny amount of paste colouring on the tip of a cocktail stick and stir until thoroughly mixed.

Flavour variations

Lemon or orange – replace the water with lemon or orange juice and add a little finely grated rind, if liked.

Coffee – replace the water with coffee essence or cold strong black coffee.

Chocolate – replace 25 g/1 oz of the icing sugar with cocoa powder.

Almond or vanilla – replace ½ teaspoon of the water with ½ teaspoon of almond or vanilla extract.

To feather-ice cupcakes, spoon glacé icing over the top of the cupcakes to cover completely. Spoon contrasting coloured or flavoured glacé icing into a piping bag fitted with a fine nozzle and quickly pipe parallel lines across the top. Use a cocktail stick to draw lightly across the piped lines in alternate directions to create a feathered effect.

Feather & Fan

To fan-ice cupcakes, instead of piping lines of contrasting icing, pipe 3 or 4 concentric circles. Create a fanned or spider's web effect by alternately drawing a cocktail stick through the icing from the centre of the cupcake to the edge and from the edge back to the centre.

Royal Icing

Royal icing is a smooth, fluid icing made from egg white and icing sugar. It's perfect for piping intricate decorations as it holds its shape well and sets hard. It's also useful for attaching decorations to fondant icing or for making pretty run-out designs to decorate cupcakes.

**MAKES ABOUT
165 G/5¾ OZ**

2 tbsp egg white

150 g/5½ oz icing sugar, sifted

a few drops of lemon juice (optional)

Step 1

Place the egg white in a bowl and, using a fork, whisk until just frothy.

Step 2

Using an electric mixer or wooden spoon, gradually beat in the icing sugar until the mixture is stiff and stands up in peaks when the beaters or spoon are lifted. To get the desired consistency for piping, beat in a few drops of lemon juice.

♡ A few drops of glycerine added with the lemon juice will stop the icing from setting too hard.

♡ Once made, royal icing will keep for a few days as long as the surface is closely covered with clingfilm. Beat thoroughly before using and add a few drops of warm water to loosen the icing if necessary.

♡ Royal icing is best coloured with food colouring pastes as liquids will affect the piping consistency. Add colouring paste sparingly with a cocktail stick and beat well.

Chocolate Ganache

Chocolate ganache is the ultimate chocolate icing for cupcakes. Made from good-quality plain chocolate and double cream, it has a beautifully glossy sheen and is ideal for piping in large swirls on top of cupcakes.

TOPS 12 CUPCAKES

150 g/5½ oz plain chocolate

200 ml/7 fl oz double cream

Step 1

Finely chop the chocolate and place in a heatproof bowl. Heat the cream in a small saucepan until almost at boiling point. Pour the cream over the chocolate.

Step 2

Stir until the chocolate has melted and the mixture is smooth.

♡ For a pouring glaze to cover the tops of cupcakes, use immediately.

♡ For spreading, allow the ganache to cool for 15–20 minutes, stirring occasionally, until thickened.

♡ For a firmer piping consistency, leave to cool for 5 minutes, then beat with an electric mixer until the ganache has cooled and thickened and is the consistency of softened butter.

♡ To make small truffles to decorate cupcakes, chill the cooled ganache until firm. Roll into tiny balls and dust with cocoa powder or icing sugar.

Piping Techniques & Tips

Whether it's big bold swirls of frosting or delicate designs in royal icing, piping turns a simple cupcake into something special.

♡ Piping nozzles

For piping buttercream, whipped cream or cream cheese frostings, you will need large metal or plastic nozzles with plain or star tips. Wide tips will allow the frosting to come out more quickly and produce big swirls.

For piping royal or glacé icing, use small metal nozzles with fine tips. You'll need one with a small plain tip for piping fine lines, dots, lettering and lacy patterns, and a star-tipped nozzle for piping shells, stars and rope patterns.

♡ Piping bags

Whether you choose to use reusable or disposable piping bags, make sure to suit the size of the bag to the quantity of frosting or icing you are using.

For piping cream, meringue, buttercream and other frostings, use large bags that allow plenty of room for filling. Don't over-fill the bag – you need to leave enough space at the top to twist it tightly closed to contain the frosting.

For royal or glacé icing, use a small or medium-sized bag. Disposable or paper piping bags are handy if you have a number of different-coloured icings on the go at one time.

Making a paper piping bag

Take a 25-cm/10-inch square of greaseproof paper. Fold it diagonally in half and cut into 2 triangles. Take 1 triangle and hold the 2 points at each end of the long edge. Curl 1 point over to meet the centre point making a cone shape, then curl the other point over so all 3 points meet. Fold the points over a few times to secure the cone. Snip off the end and use with or without a piping nozzle.

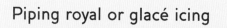

Piping royal or glacé icing

Lines and lettering – use a small bag with a fine writing nozzle. Place the tip of nozzle on the surface to be iced and squeeze the bag gently. As the icing comes out of the nozzle, lift the bag so the icing falls in a straight line or curve on the surface. To finish piping, stop squeezing and gently press the tip of the nozzle on the surface to neatly end the line of icing.

Cornelli/lace effect – use a small bag with a fine writing nozzle. Starting at an outer edge, pipe a random meandering line of icing all over the surface of the cupcake. Try not to let the lines touch or cross and keep even pressure on the piping bag so the lines are of the same thickness.

Shop-bought Decorations

☆ **Sugar sprinkles** – the simplest and easiest way to give frosted or iced cupcakes a touch of colourful fun, sugar sprinkles are readily available in a huge variety of colours, shapes and sizes. From classic hundreds and thousands to small shimmering pearls, pastel-coloured flower shapes or tiny red hearts, there's a sprinkle to suit any occasion! Always add sprinkles before the icing or frosting has set, otherwise they will drop off.

☆ **Sanding or glimmering sugar** – these are coarse sugars with grains about 4 times larger than granulated sugar that won't dissolve. You can buy them in a range of pastel or vibrant colours. They add a stylish sparkle when sprinkled over iced cupcakes.

☆ **Edible glitter** – available in tiny pots from cake decorating suppliers, a little edible glitter can really add the finishing touch to cupcakes for special occasions. Lightly sprinkle over an iced cupcake or use a fine paint brush to brush onto sugar paste or piped decorations. Use sparingly.

☆ **Sweets and chocolates** – small sweets and chocolates are great for jazzing up frosted cupcakes. Chocolate buttons, jelly beans, candy-covered chocolates and gummi bears are all ideal for children's party cupcakes and a sprinkling of popping candy just before serving will make them extra special!

☆ **Sugar flowers and shapes** – simple sugar flowers, animal faces or themed seasonal shapes are ideal to have in the storecupboard for last-minute decorations.

☆ **Fresh fruit** – for a refreshing and delicious alternative to sweet sugary sprinkles, use fresh fruit to decorate cupcakes. Try grapes, small summer berries or slices of mango, pineapple, peach or apricot. Arrange on the frosting or icing just before serving and eat on the day of topping.

☆ **Crystallized rose petals or violets** – delicately perfumed and with a crisp sugary coating, a single deep pink rose petal or purple violet will look stunning on top of a simply iced cupcake.

☆ **Nuts** – finely chopped, toasted, whole, halved or flaked, nuts are a quick and easy way to decorate a cupcake and can complement a flavouring or frosting. To lightly toast nuts, spread on a baking tray and place in a hot oven for a few minutes until light golden, or pop under a hot grill. Always store nuts in a cool dry place and check the use by date as they can go rancid if kept for too long.

The cherry on the cake

☆**Coconut** – desiccated, flaked or shredded coconut is another quick and effective decoration for cupcakes. Use lightly toasted for an extra-nutty flavour.

☆**Dragées** – these tiny and shiny edible balls are classic cupcake decorations. They are available in a variety of shimmering colours, including silver, gold, pink, blue and green. You can also buy large silver balls or heart-shaped dragées.

☆**Fresh flowers and herbs** – for a lovely summery decoration, try topping cupcakes with fresh flowers. Make absolutely sure that the flower is edible and wash carefully in cold water, then leave to dry on kitchen paper in a cool place before using. Place either the whole flower or a few petals on the cupcake just before serving. Herbs, such as mint and lemon balm, also make pretty decorations, especially when used with fresh or sugar-frosted fruit.

☆**Candied citrus peel** – with a firm and slightly grainy texture, candied lemon, orange or citron peel can be chopped or cut into thin strips to decorate iced cupcakes. For a more striking decoration, dip very thin strips of peel in melted plain chocolate and leave to set on a cooling rack, then arrange a few strips on each cupcake.

☆**Non-edible decorations** – candles and indoor sparklers make great last-minute decorations, especially for birthday or special-occasion cupcakes. Small plastic figurines or shapes can also be used to suit an event, but do remind everyone they are not edible and must be removed before eating the cupcake.

Decorating with Chocolate

Chocolate is perfect for making simple or elaborate decorations to adorn cupcakes.

♡ Melting chocolate

Break the chocolate into pieces and place in a large heatproof bowl. Set the bowl over a pan of simmering water, making sure the bowl does not touch the water, and leave until the chocolate has melted. Remove the bowl from the pan and stir the chocolate until smooth.

Take care not to let any drips of condensation come into contact with the melting chocolate or it will become grainy and 'seize' into solid lumps. For the same reason, if a recipe calls for melting chocolate with a liquid, such as milk, cream or alcohol, then add the liquid to the bowl before you start the melting process.

To melt chocolate in the microwave, break the pieces into a bowl and microwave for 1–2 minutes at a time on a medium setting until almost completely melted. Remove from the microwave and leave to stand for 2 minutes, then stir until smooth. If there are any lumps remaining, microwave for another 30 seconds–1 minute.

♡ Making chocolate caraque

Spread melted plain, milk or white chocolate in a thin and even layer onto a flat marble slab or a clean smooth surface. Leave until just set but not completely solid. Drag a thin-bladed sharp knife across the surface of the chocolate to scrape away long or short curls.

If the chocolate breaks rather than curls, it is too cold. If it sticks to the knife, it has not set enough.

♡ Making simple chocolate curls or shavings

Leave a chunky bar of chocolate at room temperature for at least an hour to soften a little. Run a swivel-headed vegetable peeler along the side of the bar of chocolate to shave off small curls or fine shavings.

♡ Making chocolate leaves ♡

Fresh leaves with well defined veins, such as bay, rose, mint and holly, are best to use. Make sure they are thoroughly clean and dry. Brush the underside of each leaf thickly with melted chocolate, taking care not to let the chocolate go over the edges of the leaves. If you are using holly leaves, don't let the chocolate drip over the prickly points. Place the leaves chocolate-side up on a sheet of baking paper and leave in a cool place until set. Carefully peel away the leaves from the chocolate. It's worth making more than you need as they are quite fragile.

♡ Making piped chocolate shapes ♡

Line a tray with baking paper. Spoon melted chocolate into a paper piping bag and snip off the very end tip of the bag. Pipe simple shapes, such as flowers, swirls or motifs, onto the paper. Don't make them too intricate or they will be too fragile. Leave in a cool place until set, then carefully peel the paper away from the chocolate. Use a small palette knife to move the shapes as the warmth of your fingers will melt the finely piped chocolate.

Decorating with Fondant Icing

Ready-to-roll fondant icing (also known as sugar paste) is a soft and pliable icing that is readily available from most supermarkets. You'll find packs of white or ivory sugar paste in most supermarkets, and ready-coloured versions are available in specialist stores.

Colouring fondant icing

It's best to use a food colouring paste to colour fondant icing as liquid will make it sticky. First, knead the icing until smooth. Smear a little food colouring from the end of a cocktail stick onto the icing, then knead the icing until you have an even colour. Add a little more colouring until you get the desired depth of colour. Wrap the icing tightly in clingfilm to prevent it from drying out.

To marble fondant icing, knead 2 different colours of fondant icing lightly together. To achieve the best effect, use about one third of a deeply coloured icing and two thirds of much paler colour or white icing and take care not to over-knead.

Rolling out fondant icing

Lightly dust a clean work surface with icing sugar and knead the icing until smooth. Using a small rolling pin (a non-stick one is best), roll out thinly, lifting and turning the icing occasionally to prevent it from sticking.

Cutting out shapes

To top cupcakes with a round of fondant icing, use a round or fluted cutter that is roughly the size of the top of the cupcake. Stamp the cutter firmly onto the rolled-out icing, twisting it slightly. Brush or spread a little jam, chocolate spread, or glacé or royal icing on the top of the cupcake. Lift the round of icing with a palette knife and gently place on top of the cupcake.

For small shapes, such as stars, hearts, letters, numbers and flowers, roll out a small amount of fondant icing. Stamp out the required shapes and carefully lift with a small angled palette knife. To attach the shapes to fondant-topped cupcakes, use a dab of water, or glacé or royal icing to stick them into place.

To dry small shapes for decoration, place on a sheet of baking paper and leave in a cool place for at least 24 hours. Once firm, they can be placed at angles on top of frosted cupcakes.

Fun with shapes!

Moulding shapes

Using small pieces of fondant icing you can mould simple shapes to decorate cupcakes. Lightly dust your hands with icing sugar to prevent the icing from sticking to them.

Decorating with Marzipan

This pliable almond paste can be used in the same way as fondant icing to decorate cupcakes, but it has a slightly moister texture, which makes it a bit trickier to colour and roll out thinly.

When colouring marzipan, use the white variety and take care not to add too much colouring as it will become sticky.

Making marzipan or fondant flowers

Roll 6 or 7 pea-sized pieces of marzipan or fondant icing in the palm of your hand into balls.

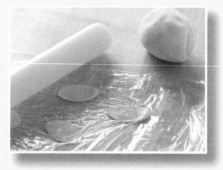

Place the balls between 2 sheets of clingfilm and flatten with a small rolling pin to make petal shapes.

Place a marble-sized piece of marzipan or fondant icing on a small board and shape into a pointed cone for the base of the rose.

Take 1 of the petals and gently wrap around the cone base to form a bud.

Continue wrapping the petals around the bud to create a rose, squeezing the base of the rose gently to make the petals curl out.

Use a sharp knife to cut the rose away from the base and leave to dry in a cool place.

To dust the edges with edible glitter, use a fine paintbrush to lightly brush the tops of the petals with a little water. Dip into edible glitter, then gently tap the roses on a sheet of kitchen paper to remove any excess glitter. Leave in a cool place until dry.

Pretty as a picture

Sugar Frosting Fruit, Flowers & Herbs

Choose firm berries, such as blueberries, raspberries, redcurrants and strawberries, or small grapes. Make sure that they have no blemishes or soft patches.

Flowers or single petals should be clean and edible (see below). Rose petals work especially well.

Leafy herbs, such as mint, lemon balm and bay, are ideal for sugar frosting or try small sprigs of fresh thyme or marjoram.

Using a small paintbrush, lightly brush the fruit, flowers, petals or leaves all over with a little beaten egg white, making sure to coat the underside of leaves and petals.

Coat flowers with sugar by holding over a plate and sprinkling liberally with caster sugar, shaking off any excess sugar. To coat leaves, petals and berries, place the sugar on a flat plate and either dip or roll in the sugar to coat.

Place on a sheet of baking paper or cooling rack and leave in cool place for a few hours or overnight until dry. Soft berry fruits will only keep for a day but grapes, leaves and flowers will keep for 2–3 days stored in a cool dry place.

Edible flowers

Roses Lavender

Marigolds Pansies

Nasturtiums

Building Cupcake Shapes

By stacking different-sized cupcakes on top of each other you can create large fun novelty cupcakes, such as the Ghostly Ghoul Cupcakes (see page 212). You can also build up 3D shapes with mini doughnuts, marshmallows, ice-cream cones or rolled balls of fondant icing or marzipan.

To make sure the stacked shapes stick together, spread with plenty of buttercream or icing. Chill the assembled cupcake until the icing is firm before covering in fondant icing or frosting.

More ideas for shaped cupcakes

Christmas trees – follow the same stacking method as for the Ghostly Ghoul Cupcakes, but shape the balls of fondant icing into triangular points to resemble the tops of the trees. Spread or pipe all over with green-coloured buttercream and dot with silver dragées.

Witches' hats – spread a raised mound of green buttercream over the top of each cupcake. Place a small inverted waffle ice-cream cone on top of each to resemble a witch's hat. Use tubes of writing icing to pipe eyes, a nose and straggly black hair under the hat.

Beehives – top each cupcake with another upturned cupcake. Using a large plain piping nozzle, pipe lines of honey-flavoured buttercream all around the raised cupcakes to create a beehive effect. Decorate with fondant bees and flowers.

Making your Cupcakes Special

Edging and coating cupcakes

A simple way to give frosted cupcakes a colourful or decorative finish is to coat the top or edges lightly with sugar sprinkles, grated chocolate, finely chopped nuts, coloured sugar or crushed boiled sweets.

To edge cupcakes, spread the coating on a flat plate. Hold a cupcake by its base and quickly roll the raised frosted edge in the coating, shaking off any excess.

To completely coat cupcakes, smooth frosting over the cupcake in a raised mound. Hold the cupcake over a plate and liberally sprinkle with the coating, pressing down lightly with your fingers if necessary.

When using buttercream, it's best to frost and coat the cupcakes one at a time, otherwise the frosting will dry a little and the coating will not stick.

Stencilling designs on cupcakes

Simple but very effective designs can be created for the top of cupcakes using bought or home-made stencils and dusting with cocoa, icing sugar, coloured sugar or finely grated chocolate.

Small coffee stencils with simple designs, such as hearts, flowers and stars, are ideal to use. Hold steadily close to the surface of the cupcake and liberally spoon or shake over sifted cocoa, icing sugar, coloured sugar or sprinkles. Gently lift away the stencil.

Alternatively, cut out your own simple shapes from a piece of card or, to create a lacy pattern, cut a round piece of a paper doily to fit the top of the cupcake.

For a geometric design, lay thin strips of paper gently on top of the cupcake and dust liberally with icing sugar or cocoa powder. Very carefully lift away the strips of paper.

Adding flavour to cupcakes

Brushing or spooning syrup over cupcakes while they are still warm from the oven will infuse them with extra flavour, as well as helping to keep them deliciously moist. This is especially useful when making a big batch of cupcakes for a special event.

To make a basic sugar syrup, place 40 g/1½ oz caster sugar and 4 tablespoons of water in a small pan and heat gently until the sugar dissolves. Boil, without stirring, for about 1 minute, until syrupy, then leave to cool for at least 10 minutes.

Use a skewer to pierce a few holes in the top of the warm cupcakes and liberally spoon or brush the syrup over the top. Leave to cool completely before topping with frosting or icing.

Syrup flavours

Lemon or orange – replace the water with lemon or orange juice.

Coffee – add 2 teaspoons of instant coffee granules.

Rum – replace 2 tablespoons of the water with dark rum.

Vanilla or almond – add 1 teaspoon of vanilla or almond extract.

Hidden fillings for cupcakes

To add a surprise element to cupcakes, try scooping out a little of the sponge and adding a sweet filling.

Suit the filling to the flavour of the cupcake. Strawberry or raspberry jam goes particularly well with vanilla or almond cupcakes. Try chocolate spread with chocolate or coffee cupcakes, and lemon curd or marmalade with citrus-flavoured cupcakes.

To scoop out the sponge, make sure the cupcake is completely cold, then use a teaspoon or the tip of a small knife to cut away a small piece of sponge. Spoon a little of the filling into the hole, taking care not to over-fill, and then place the piece of sponge back in place, pressing down gently.

The Finishing Touches

When serving cupcakes at special occasions or giving them as gifts, it's well worth taking a little time to think about the presentation or packaging. From traditional cake stands to beautiful boxes and colourful ribbons, the finishing touches make all the difference!

Cupcake flags

A quick and easy way to jazz up cupcakes for a party or special event is to decorate them with small flags. You can buy these ready-made, often themed for seasonal events, such as Christmas or Halloween, or just make your own to suit the occasion.

To make your own, cut out a small piece of thin card or paper (plain or patterned) using the template on this page as a guide. Fold around a cocktail stick and glue together the 2 halves. If liked, draw a simple design on the flags or write a message on them.

To make heart-shaped or flower-shaped cupcake flags, trace the outline of a small cookie cutter onto coloured card. Cut out carefully and, using glue or double-sided tape, stick 2 identical shapes back-to-back on a cocktail stick.

Template

Gift tags

A box of cupcakes given as a gift for a special occasion needs labelling with a pretty gift or name tag.

Gift tags are available to buy in a range of colours and sizes and you can pick them to suit the colour or flavour of cupcake being given. However, for a more personal touch why not make your own?

To make your own, choose a piece of firm paper or thin card and use one of the templates on this page as a guide to cut out the gift tag shape. Make a hole at the end or corner of the tag with a hole puncher and thread with thin ribbon or string.

Templates

Perfect Presentation

Whether you've just got friends over for a coffee or you're celebrating a more formal occasion, such as a birthday or wedding, always make your home-made cupcakes centre stage by arranging them on pretty plates or stands.

Cake plates – elegantly decorated cupcakes look even more delicious when arranged on pretty tea plates or china cake stands. Make sure that you don't position the cupcakes too close together – allow enough room so that you can take a cake from the plate or stand without damaging any of the others. Add extra decorations around the cupcakes if liked, such as small flowers, fresh herbs, sugared almonds, ribbons or small bows.

Cupcake stands – these are ideal for displaying and serving lots of cupcakes. Special metal stands with individual wired holders for each cupcake, which ensure that the frosting or icing doesn't get damaged, are ideal. Alternatively, look out for cheaper disposable cardboard stands in a variety of colours and patterns. Both types can hold between 20–30 cupcakes – enough for a party or small wedding. For a larger quantity of cupcakes, it may be worth hiring a tiered cake stand from a specialist cake supplier or make your own tiered stand using different-sized cake boards and cake pillars.

Cupcake wrappers – these decorative strips of light card come in a variety of patterns and colours and are great for wrapping around individual cupcakes. Some have themed designs while others have fancy laced or scalloped edges. They are simply wrapped around single cupcakes and sealed with a tab fastening.

Gift boxes – available in a huge range of sizes and colours, gift boxes are an ideal way to give cupcakes as presents. Look for boxes with a clear panel in the top so that you can see the contents without opening the lid. Some kitchen shops stock cupcake boxes with special inserts into which you can slot the cupcakes to hold them safely in place.

Cellophane bags – these are the perfect way to present a single cupcake as a gift. They are available in clear or patterned versions. Tie them with a pretty ribbon for an extra-special touch.

Summer Garden Cupcakes

MAKES 8

115 g/4 oz butter, softened, or soft margarine

115 g/4 oz caster sugar

2 tsp rose water

2 large eggs, lightly beaten

115 g/4 oz self-raising flour

TO DECORATE

115 g/4 oz pink ready-to-roll fondant icing

icing sugar, for dusting

85 g/3 oz white ready-to-roll fondant icing

85 g/3 oz blue ready-to-roll fondant icing

tube of yellow writing icing

BUTTERCREAM

175 g/6 oz unsalted butter, softened

6 tbsp double cream

350 g/12 oz icing sugar

green food colouring

Preheat the oven to 180°C/350°F/Gas Mark 4. Put 8 paper cases in a bun tray.

Place the butter, caster sugar and rose water in a large bowl and beat together until light and fluffy. Gradually beat in the eggs. Sift in the flour and, using a metal spoon, fold in gently.

Spoon the mixture into the paper cases. Bake in the preheated oven for 15–20 minutes, or until risen, golden and firm to the touch. Transfer to a wire rack and leave to cool.

Roll out the pink fondant icing to a thickness of 5 mm/¼ inch on a surface lightly dusted with icing sugar. Using a small butterfly cutter, stamp out 16 butterflies. Roll out the white and blue fondant icings to the same thickness and, using a small daisy cutter, stamp out about 40 flowers, re-rolling the icing as necessary. Use the yellow writing icing to pipe centres in the flowers.

To make the buttercream, place the butter in a bowl and beat with an electric mixer for 2–3 minutes, until pale and creamy. Beat in the cream, then gradually sift in the icing sugar and continue beating for 2–3 minutes, until the buttercream is light and fluffy. Beat in a little green food colouring to give a light green colour.

Spoon the buttercream into a large piping bag fitted with a large star nozzle. Pipe swirls of buttercream on top of each cupcake. Decorate with the fondant butterflies and flowers.

Rocky Road Cupcakes

MAKES 12

2 tbsp cocoa powder

2 tbsp hot water

115 g/4 oz butter, softened, or soft margarine

115 g/4 oz caster sugar

2 eggs, lightly beaten

115 g/4 oz self-raising flour

TOPPING

25 g/1 oz chopped mixed nuts

100 g/3½ oz milk chocolate, melted

115 g/4 oz mini marshmallows

40 g/1½ oz glacé cherries, chopped

Preheat the oven to 180°C/350°F/Gas Mark 4. Put 12 paper cases in a muffin tray.

Blend the cocoa powder and hot water and set aside. Place the butter and caster sugar in a large bowl and beat together until light and fluffy. Gradually beat in the eggs, then beat in the cocoa mixture. Sift in the flour and, using a metal spoon, fold in gently.

Spoon the mixture into the paper cases. Bake in the preheated oven for 20 minutes, or until risen and firm to the touch. Transfer to a wire rack and leave to cool.

To make the topping, stir the nuts into the melted chocolate and spread a little of the mixture over the top of the cupcakes. Lightly stir the marshmallows and glacé cherries into the remaining chocolate mixture and pile on top of the cupcakes. Leave to set.

'99' Cupcakes

MAKES 8

175 g/6 oz butter, softened, or soft margarine

175 g/6 oz caster sugar

3 eggs, lightly beaten

1 tsp vanilla extract

150 g/5½ oz self-raising flour

55 g/2 oz ground almonds

BUTTERCREAM

225 g/8 oz unsalted butter, softened

1 tbsp cream or milk

350 g/12 oz icing sugar

TO DECORATE

12 mini chocolate flakes

hundreds and thousands

Preheat the oven to 180°C/350°F/Gas Mark 4. Put 8 paper cases in a muffin tray.

Place the butter and caster sugar in a large bowl and beat together until light and fluffy. Gradually beat in the eggs and vanilla extract. Sift in the flour and, using a metal spoon, fold gently into the mixture with the ground almonds.

Spoon the mixture into the paper cases. Bake in the preheated oven for 20–25 minutes, or until risen, golden and firm to the touch. Transfer to a wire rack and leave to cool.

To make the buttercream, place the butter in a bowl and beat with an electric mixer for 2–3 minutes, until pale and creamy. Beat in the cream, then gradually sift in the icing sugar and continue beating for 2–3 minutes, until the buttercream is light and fluffy.

Spoon the buttercream into a large piping bag fitted with a large star nozzle. Pipe swirls of buttercream on top of each cupcake to resemble ice cream. Press a chocolate flake into each swirl of buttercream and scatter with hundreds and thousands.

Lollipop Cupcakes

MAKES 12

115 g/4 oz butter, softened, or soft margarine

115 g/4 oz caster sugar

2 tsp finely grated orange rind

2 eggs, lightly beaten

115 g/4 oz self-raising flour

BUTTERCREAM

115 g/4 oz unsalted butter, softened

2 tbsp orange juice

225 g/8 oz icing sugar

orange food colouring

TO DECORATE

85 g/3 oz green ready-to-roll fondant icing

icing sugar, for dusting

red sugar sprinkles

12 small candy lollipops

Preheat the oven to 180°C/350°F/Gas Mark 4. Put 12 paper cases in a bun tray.

Place the butter, caster sugar and orange rind in a large bowl and beat together until light and fluffy. Gradually beat in the eggs. Sift in the flour and, using a metal spoon, fold in gently.

Spoon the mixture into the paper cases. Bake in the preheated oven for 15–20 minutes, or until risen, golden and firm to the touch. Transfer to a wire rack and leave to cool.

To make the buttercream, place the butter and orange juice in a bowl and beat with an electric mixer for 2–3 minutes, until pale and creamy. Gradually sift in the icing sugar and continue beating for 2–3 minutes, until the buttercream is light and fluffy. Beat in a little orange food colouring.

Roll out the green fondant icing to a thickness of 5 mm/¼ inch on a surface lightly dusted with icing sugar. Using a small leaf cutter, stamp out 24 leaves. Swirl the buttercream on the top of the cupcakes and edge with sugar sprinkles. Place a lollipop and 2 fondant leaves in the centre of each cupcake.

Chocolate Florentine Cupcakes

MAKES 12

55 g/2 oz plain chocolate

85 g/3 oz butter, softened, or soft margarine

1 tbsp golden syrup

55 g/2 oz light soft brown sugar

115 g/4 oz self-raising flour

1 large egg, lightly beaten

TOPPING

40 g/1½ oz glacé cherries, chopped

25 g/1 oz flaked almonds

1 tbsp raisins

1 tbsp golden syrup

Preheat the oven to 190°C/375°F/Gas Mark 5. Put 12 paper cases in a bun tray.

Put the chocolate, butter, golden syrup and brown sugar in a saucepan and heat gently, stirring occasionally, until just melted. Leave to cool for 2 minutes.

Sift the flour into a large bowl and pour in the chocolate mixture. Add the egg and beat until thoroughly blended.

Spoon the mixture into the paper cases. Mix together the topping ingredients and gently spoon a little of the mixture on top of each cupcake.

Bake in the preheated oven for 15–20 minutes, or until risen and firm to the touch. Transfer to a wire rack and leave to cool.

Cream Tea Cupcakes

MAKES 10

85 g/3 oz butter, softened, or soft margarine

85 g/3 oz caster sugar

1 large egg, lightly beaten

½ tsp vanilla extract

85 g/3 oz self-raising flour

1 tbsp milk

40 g/1½ oz raisins

TO DECORATE

115 g/4 oz small strawberries, hulled and sliced

1 tbsp strawberry jam

115 g/4 oz clotted cream

icing sugar, for dusting

Preheat the oven to 190°C/375°F/Gas Mark 5. Put 10 paper cases in a bun tray.

Place the butter and caster sugar in a large bowl and beat together until light and fluffy. Gradually beat in the egg and vanilla extract. Sift in the flour and, using a metal spoon, fold gently into the mixture with the milk and raisins.

Spoon the mixture into the paper cases. Bake in the preheated oven for 15–20 minutes, or until risen, golden and firm to the touch. Transfer to a wire rack and leave to cool.

Use a serrated knife to cut a circle from the top of each cupcake. Gently mix together the strawberries and jam and divide among the cupcakes. Top each with a small dollop of clotted cream. Replace the cupcake tops and dust with icing sugar.

Feather-iced Coffee Cupcakes

MAKES 16

115 g/4 oz self-raising flour

½ tsp baking powder

115 g/4 oz butter, softened, or soft margarine

115 g/4 oz soft light brown sugar

2 eggs, lightly beaten

1 tbsp instant coffee granules dissolved in 1 tbsp boiling water, cooled

2 tbsp soured cream

ICING

225 g/8 oz icing sugar

4 tsp warm water

1 tbsp instant coffee granules dissolved in 2 tbsp boiling water

Preheat the oven to 190°C/375°F/Gas Mark 5. Put 16 paper cases in bun trays.

Sift the flour and baking powder into a large bowl. Add the butter, brown sugar and eggs and, using an electric mixer, beat together until smooth. Beat in the dissolved coffee and soured cream.

Spoon the mixture into the paper cases. Bake in the preheated oven for 20 minutes, or until risen, golden and firm to the touch. Transfer to a wire rack and leave to cool.

To make the icing, sift 85 g/3 oz of the icing sugar into a bowl, then gradually mix in the water. Sift the remaining icing sugar into a separate bowl, then stir in the dissolved coffee.

Spoon the coffee icing into a piping bag fitted with a fine nozzle. Spoon the white icing over the cupcakes to cover completely. Quickly pipe parallel lines of the coffee icing across the top. Use a cocktail stick to draw lightly across the piped lines in alternate directions to create a feathered effect.

Lemon Butterfly Cupcakes

MAKES 12

115 g/4 oz self-raising flour

½ tsp baking powder

115 g/4 oz butter, softened, or soft margarine

115 g/4 oz caster sugar

2 eggs, lightly beaten

finely grated rind of ½ lemon

2 tbsp milk

BUTTERCREAM

85 g/3 oz unsalted butter, softened

175/6 oz icing sugar, plus extra for dusting

1 tbsp lemon juice

Preheat the oven to 190°C/375°F/Gas Mark 5. Put 12 paper cases in a bun tray.

Sift the flour and baking powder into a large bowl. Add the butter, caster sugar, eggs, lemon rind and milk and, using an electric mixer, beat together until smooth.

Spoon the mixture into the paper cases. Bake in the preheated oven for 15–20 minutes, or until risen, golden and firm to the touch. Transfer to a wire rack and leave to cool.

To make the buttercream, put the butter in a bowl and beat until fluffy. Sift in the icing sugar, add the lemon juice and beat together until smooth and creamy.

Use a serrated knife to cut a circle from the top of each cupcake, then cut each circle in half. Spread or pipe a little of the buttercream onto the centre of each cupcake, then press 2 semicircular halves into it at an angle to resemble butterfly wings. Dust with icing sugar.

Jammy Cupcakes

MAKES 28

175 g/6 oz plain flour

1 tbsp baking powder

1 tbsp custard powder

175 g/6 oz butter, softened, or soft margarine

175 g/6 oz caster sugar

3 eggs, lightly beaten

1 tsp vanilla extract

70 g/2½ oz raspberry jam

icing sugar, for dusting

Preheat the oven to 190°C/375°F/Gas Mark 5. Put 28 paper cases into bun trays.

Sift the flour, baking powder and custard powder into a large bowl. Add the butter, caster sugar, eggs and vanilla extract and, using an electric mixer, beat together until smooth.

Spoon the mixture into the paper cases and place ½ teaspoon of the jam onto the centre of each, without pressing down.

Bake in the preheated oven for 15–20 minutes, or until risen, golden and firm to the touch. Transfer to a wire rack and leave to cool. Dust with icing sugar.

Ladybird Cupcakes

MAKES 10

115 g/4 oz self-raising flour

½ tsp baking powder

115 g/4 oz butter, softened, or soft margarine

115 g/4 oz caster sugar

2 large eggs, lightly beaten

85 g/3 oz milk chocolate, melted

1 tbsp milk

TO DECORATE

225 g/8 oz red ready-to-roll fondant icing

icing sugar, for dusting

2 tbsp raspberry jam

85 g/3 oz black ready-to-roll fondant icing

tubes of black and white writing icing

Preheat the oven to 180°C/350°F/Gas Mark 4. Put 10 paper cases in a muffin tray.

Sift the flour and baking powder into a large bowl. Add the butter, caster sugar and eggs and, using an electric mixer, beat together until smooth. Beat in the melted chocolate and milk.

Spoon the mixture into the paper cases. Bake in the preheated oven for 18–22 minutes, until risen and firm to the touch. Transfer to a wire rack and leave to cool.

Roll out the red fondant icing to a thickness of 5 mm/ ¼ inch on a surface lightly dusted with icing sugar. Using a 7-cm/2¾-inch round cutter, stamp out 10 rounds, re-rolling the icing as necessary. Brush each cupcake lightly with a little of the jam and gently press an icing round on top. Roll out the black fondant icing to the same thickness and cut out 10 ovals for the ladybird faces. Lightly brush with water and press on top of the red icing.

Shape the trimmings from the black fondant icing into small spots and attach with a dab of water. Use the black writing icing to pipe a line to divide the wings and 2 small antennae on each cupcake. Use the white writing icing to pipe eyes and a smile onto the face of each ladybird. Dot the eyes with tiny rolled balls of black fondant icing.

Marbled Chocolate Cupcakes

MAKES 21

175 g/6 oz self-raising flour

175 g/6 oz butter, softened, or soft margarine

175 g/6 oz caster sugar

3 eggs, lightly beaten

2 tbsp milk

55 g/2 oz plain chocolate, melted

Preheat the oven to 180°C/350°F/Gas Mark 4. Put 21 paper cases in bun trays.

Sift the flour into a large bowl. Add the butter, caster sugar, eggs and milk and, using an electric mixer, beat together until smooth.

Divide the mixture between 2 bowls. Add the melted chocolate to 1 of the bowls and stir until well mixed. Place alternate teaspoonfuls of the mixtures into the paper cases.

Bake in the preheated oven for 20 minutes, or until risen and firm to the touch. Transfer to a wire rack and leave to cool.

Pink & White Cupcakes

MAKES 16

115 g/4 oz self-raising flour

1 tsp baking powder

115 g/4 oz butter, softened, or soft margarine

115 g/4 oz caster sugar

2 eggs, lightly beaten

1 tbsp milk

red food colouring (optional)

TOPPING

1 egg white

175 g/6 oz caster sugar

2 tbsp hot water

large pinch of cream of tartar

2 tbsp raspberry jam

2 tbsp lightly toasted desiccated coconut

Preheat the oven to 180°C/350°F/Gas Mark 4. Put 16 paper cases in bun trays.

Sift the flour and baking powder into a large bowl. Add the butter, caster sugar and eggs and, using an electric mixer, beat together until smooth. Mix together the milk and a little red food colouring, if using, and beat into the mixture until evenly blended.

Spoon the mixture into the paper cases. Bake in the preheated oven for 20 minutes, or until risen, golden and firm to the touch. Transfer to a wire rack and leave to cool.

Put the egg white, caster sugar, water and cream of tartar in a heatproof bowl set over a saucepan of simmering water. Using an electric mixer, beat for 5–6 minutes, until the mixture is thick and softly peaks when the whisk is lifted.

Spread a layer of jam over each cupcake, then swirl over the frosting. Sprinkle with the desiccated coconut.

Cheeky Monkey Cupcakes

MAKES 12

115 g/4 oz butter, softened, or soft margarine

85 g/3 oz soft light brown sugar

1 tbsp honey

2 eggs, lightly beaten

100 g/3½ oz self-raising flour

2 tbsp cocoa powder

TO DECORATE

350 g/12 oz ivory ready-to-roll fondant icing

brown food colouring

icing sugar, for dusting

2 tbsp chocolate spread

24 large chocolate buttons

tubes of white and black writing icing

12 brown candy-covered chocolate beans

Preheat the oven to 180°C/350°F/Gas Mark 4. Put 12 paper cases in a bun tray.

Place the butter, brown sugar and honey in a large bowl and beat together until light and fluffy. Gradually beat in the eggs. Sift in the flour and cocoa powder and, using a metal spoon, fold in gently.

Spoon the mixture into the paper cases. Bake in the preheated oven for 15–20 minutes, until risen and firm to the touch. Transfer to a wire rack and leave to cool.

Colour two thirds of the ivory fondant icing pale brown with a little brown food colouring. Roll out the brown fondant icing to a thickness of 5 mm/¼ inch on a surface lightly dusted with icing sugar. Using a 7-cm/2¾-inch round cutter, stamp out 12 rounds. Roll out the remaining ivory fondant icing to the same thickness and, using the end of a large plain piping nozzle, cut out 24 small rounds. Re-roll the icing and cut out 12 ovals.

Spread the top of the cupcakes with a thin layer of chocolate spread and top with the rounds of brown icing. Attach 2 ivory rounds and 1 oval on top of each cupcake with a little water to resemble a monkey's face. Arrange 2 chocolate buttons on the side of each cupcake for ears and attach with some of the writing icing. Use the white and black writing icings to pipe eyes and a mouth and place a chocolate bean in the centre of each face for a nose.

Black Forest Cupcakes

MAKES 12

1 tsp lemon juice

4 tbsp milk

150 g/5½ oz self-raising flour

1 tbsp cocoa powder

½ tsp bicarbonate of soda

2 eggs, lightly beaten

55 g/2 oz butter, softened, or soft margarine

115 g/4 oz soft light brown sugar

85 g/3 oz plain chocolate, melted

25 g/1 oz dried and sweetened sour cherries, chopped

TO DECORATE

2 tbsp cherry liqueur (optional)

150 ml/5 fl oz double cream, softly whipped

5 tbsp cherry jam

cocoa powder, for dusting

Preheat the oven to 180°C/350°F/Gas Mark 4. Put 12 paper cases in a muffin tray.

Add the lemon juice to the milk and leave for 10 minutes – the milk will curdle a little.

Sift the flour, cocoa powder and bicarbonate of soda into a large bowl. Add the eggs, butter, brown sugar and milk mixture and, using an electric mixer, beat until smooth. Fold in the melted chocolate and sour cherries.

Spoon the mixture into the paper cases. Bake in the preheated oven for 20–25 minutes, or until risen and firm to the touch. Transfer to a wire rack and leave to cool.

Cut a circle from the top of each cupcake. Sprinkle the cupcakes with the cherry liqueur, if using. Spoon the whipped cream onto the centres and top with a small spoonful of jam. Gently replace the cupcake tops and dust lightly with cocoa powder.

Lemon Meringue Cupcakes

MAKES 4

85 g/3 oz butter, softened, or soft margarine, plus extra for greasing

85 g/3 oz caster sugar

finely grated rind and juice of ½ lemon

1 large egg, lightly beaten

85 g/3 oz self-raising flour

2 tbsp lemon curd

MERINGUE

2 egg whites

115 g/4 oz caster sugar

Preheat the oven to 190°C/375°F/Gas Mark 5. Grease 4 x 200-ml/7-fl oz ovenproof teacups or ramekins.

Place the butter, caster sugar and lemon rind in a large bowl and beat together until light and fluffy. Gradually beat in the egg. Sift in the flour and, using a metal spoon, fold into the mixture with the lemon juice.

Spoon the mixture into the teacups or ramekins. Put the teacups or ramekins on a baking sheet. Bake in the preheated oven for 15 minutes, or until risen, golden and firm to the touch.

While the cupcakes are baking, make the meringue. Put the egg whites in a grease-free bowl and, using a electric mixer, whisk until stiff. Gradually whisk in the caster sugar to form a stiff and glossy meringue.

Spread the lemon curd over the hot cupcakes, then swirl over the meringue. Return the cupcakes to the oven for 4–5 minutes, until the meringue is golden. Serve immediately.

Bouquet of Cupcakes

MAKES 16

140 g/5 oz self-raising flour

¼ tsp baking powder

115 g/4 oz butter, softened, or soft margarine

115 g/4 oz caster sugar

2 eggs, lightly beaten

½ vanilla pod

2 tbsp milk

BUTTERCREAM

175 g/6 oz unsalted butter, softened

1 tsp vanilla extract

350 g/12 oz icing sugar

pink and purple food colourings

TO ASSEMBLE

12-cm/4½-inch cube of floral foam (oasis)

white and pink tissue paper

15-cm/6-inch terracotta pot

cocktail sticks

fresh bay leaves

ribbon

Preheat the oven to 180°C/350°F/Gas Mark 4. Put 16 paper cases in bun trays.

Sift the flour and baking powder into a large bowl. Add the butter, caster sugar, eggs, seeds from the vanilla pod and milk and, using an electric mixer, beat together until smooth.

Spoon the mixture into the paper cases. Bake in the preheated oven for 15–20 minutes, until risen, golden and firm to the touch. Transfer to a wire rack and leave to cool.

To make the buttercream, place the butter and vanilla extract in a bowl and beat with an electric mixer for 2–3 minutes, until pale and creamy. Gradually sift in the icing sugar and continue beating for 2–3 minutes, until light and fluffy. Divide between 2 bowls and beat a little pink food colouring into 1 of the bowls and a little purple food colouring into the other.

Spoon each buttercream into a large piping bag fitted with a medium star nozzle. Pipe swirls of pink buttercream over 8 of the cupcakes and purple buttercream over the remaining 8. Chill for 30 minutes.

To assemble, use a sharp knife to trim off the corners of the cube of floral foam. Wrap in a layer of white tissue paper and press into the terracotta pot. Push 2 cocktail sticks into the base of each cupcake and gently push the cupcakes into the floral foam. Place a few bay leaves in between the cupcakes. Wrap the pot in pink tissue paper and tie with ribbon.

Frosted Berry Cupcakes

MAKES 12

115 g/4 oz butter,
softened, or soft
margarine

115 g/4 oz caster sugar

2 tsp orange flower water

2 large eggs, lightly beaten

55 g/2 oz ground almonds

115 g/4 oz self-raising
flour

2 tbsp milk

FROSTING

300 g/10½ oz mascarpone
cheese

85 g/3 oz caster sugar

4 tbsp orange juice

TO DECORATE

280 g/10 oz sugar-frosted
mixed berries
(see page 42)

a few sugar-frosted fresh
mint leaves (see page 42)

Preheat the oven to 180°C/350°F/Gas Mark 4. Put 12 paper cases in a bun tray.

Place the butter, caster sugar and orange flower water in a large bowl and beat together until light and fluffy. Gradually beat in the eggs. Stir in the ground almonds. Sift in the flour and, using a metal spoon, fold in gently with the milk.

Spoon the mixture into the paper cases. Bake in the preheated oven for 15–20 minutes, until risen, golden and firm to the touch. Transfer to a wire rack and leave to cool.

To make the frosting, put the mascarpone, caster sugar and orange juice in a bowl and beat together until smooth.

Swirl the frosting over the top of the cupcakes and arrange the sugar-frosted berries and mint leaves on top.

87

Gooey Chocolate & Cream Cheese Cupcakes

MAKES 12

175 g/6 oz plain flour

20 g/³/₄ oz cocoa powder

³/₄ tsp bicarbonate of soda

200 g/7 oz caster sugar

50 ml/2 fl oz sunflower oil

175 ml/6 fl oz water

2 tsp white vinegar

¹/₂ tsp vanilla extract

150 g/5¹/₂ oz full-fat cream cheese

1 egg, lightly beaten

100 g/3¹/₂ oz plain chocolate chips

Preheat the oven to 180°C/350°F/Gas Mark 4. Put 12 paper cases in a muffin tray.

Sift the flour, cocoa powder and bicarbonate of soda into a large bowl. Stir 150 g/5¹/₂ oz of the caster sugar into the flour mixture. Add the oil, water, vinegar and vanilla extract and stir well until combined.

Place the remaining caster sugar, the cream cheese and egg in a large bowl and beat together until well mixed. Stir in the chocolate chips.

Spoon the cake mixture into the paper cases and top each with a spoonful of the cream cheese mixture. Bake in the preheated oven for 20–25 minutes, or until risen and firm to the touch. Transfer to a wire rack and leave to cool.

Caramel Cupcakes

MAKES 12

85 g/3 oz butter, softened, or soft margarine

55 g/2 oz soft dark brown sugar

1 tbsp golden syrup

1 large egg, lightly beaten

100 g/3½ oz self-raising flour

1 tsp freshly grated nutmeg

2 tbsp milk

TOPPING

115 g/4 oz soft light brown sugar

1 small egg white

1 tbsp hot water

pinch of cream of tartar

Preheat the oven to 180°C/350°F/Gas Mark 4. Put 12 paper cases in a bun tray.

Place the butter, dark brown sugar and golden syrup in a large bowl and beat together until light and fluffy. Gradually beat in the egg. Sift in the flour and nutmeg and, using a metal spoon, fold gently into the mixture with the milk.

Spoon the mixture into the paper cases. Bake in the preheated oven for 15–20 minutes, or until risen, golden and firm to the touch. Transfer to a wire rack and leave to cool.

To make the topping, put all the ingredients in a heatproof bowl set over a saucepan of simmering water. Using an electric mixer, beat for 5–6 minutes, until the mixture is thick and softly peaking when the whisk is lifted. Swirl the topping over the cupcakes.

Red Velvet Cupcakes

MAKES 12

140 g/5 oz plain flour

1 tsp bicarbonate of soda

2 tbsp cocoa powder

115 g/4 oz butter, softened, or soft margarine

140 g/5 oz caster sugar

1 large egg, lightly beaten

125 ml/4 fl oz buttermilk

1 tsp vanilla extract

1 tbsp red food colouring liquid

FROSTING

140 g/5 oz full-fat cream cheese

85 g/3 oz unsalted butter, softened

280 g/10 oz icing sugar

TO DECORATE

55 g/2 oz granulated sugar

red food colouring paste

Preheat the oven to 180°C/350°F/Gas Mark 4. Put 12 paper cases in a bun tray.

Sift together the flour, bicarbonate of soda and cocoa powder. Place the butter and caster sugar in a separate large bowl and beat together until light and fluffy. Gradually beat in the egg and half the flour mixture. Beat in the buttermilk, vanilla extract and red food colouring. Fold in the remaining flour mixture.

Spoon the mixture into the paper cases. Bake the cupcakes in the preheated oven for 15–20 minutes, or until risen and firm to the touch. Transfer to a wire rack and leave to cool.

To make the frosting, put the cream cheese and butter in a bowl and blend together with a spatula. Sift in the icing sugar and beat until smooth and creamy.

Place the granulated sugar and a little red food colouring paste in a plastic bag. Rub the bag between your fingers and thumb until well mixed. Swirl the frosting on the top of the cupcakes and sprinkle with the coloured sugar.

Fudge & Raisin Cupcakes

MAKES 10

115 g/4 oz vanilla fudge, cut into small chunks

1 tbsp milk

85 g/3 oz butter, softened, or soft margarine

40 g/1½ oz soft light brown sugar

1 large egg, lightly beaten

100 g/3½ oz self-raising flour

25 g/1 oz raisins

Preheat the oven to 190°C/375°F/Gas Mark 5. Put 10 paper cases in a bun tray.

Put half the fudge in a heatproof bowl with the milk, set over a saucepan of gently simmering water and leave until the fudge has melted. Remove from the heat and stir until smooth. Leave to cool for 10 minutes.

Place the butter and brown sugar into a large bowl and beat together until light and fluffy. Gradually beat in the egg. Sift in the flour and, using a metal spoon, fold gently into the mixture with the raisins. Fold in the melted fudge.

Spoon the mixture into the paper cases. Scatter the remaining fudge chunks over the cupcakes. Bake in the preheated oven for 15–20 minutes, or until risen, golden and firm to the touch. Transfer to a wire rack and leave to cool.

Gingerbread Cupcakes

MAKES 30

175 g/6 oz plain flour

1 tbsp baking powder

2 tsp ground ginger

1 tsp ground cinnamon

175 g/6 oz butter, softened, or soft margarine

175 g/6 oz dark muscovado sugar

3 eggs, lightly beaten

1 tsp vanilla extract

chopped crystallized ginger, to decorate

BUTTERCREAM

85 g/3 oz unsalted butter, softened

3 tbsp orange juice

150 g/5½ oz icing sugar

Preheat the oven to 190°C/375°F/Gas Mark 5. Put 30 paper cases into bun trays.

Sift the flour, baking powder, ground ginger and cinnamon into a large bowl. Add the butter, muscovado sugar, eggs and vanilla extract and, using an electric mixer, beat together until smooth.

Spoon the mixture into the paper cases. Bake in the preheated oven for 15–20 minutes, or until risen, golden and firm to the touch. Transfer the to a wire rack and leave to cool.

To make the buttercream, place the butter and orange juice in a bowl and beat with an electric mixer until smooth. Sift in the icing sugar and continue beating until light and fluffy. Spoon a little of the buttercream on top of each cupcake and scatter over the crystallized ginger.

Cherry Sundae Cupcakes

MAKES 12

175 g/6 oz butter, softened, or soft margarine

175 g/6 oz caster sugar

3 eggs, lightly beaten

1 tsp vanilla extract

200 g/7 oz plain flour

1½ tsp baking powder

55 g/2 oz glacé cherries, chopped

CHOCOLATE SAUCE

85 g/3 oz plain chocolate, broken into pieces

25 g/1 oz butter

1 tbsp golden syrup

TO DECORATE

600 ml/1 pint double cream

2 tbsp toasted chopped mixed nuts

pink glimmer sugar

12 maraschino cherries

Preheat the oven to 160°C/325°F/Gas Mark 3. Put 12 paper cases in a muffin tray.

Place the butter and caster sugar in a large bowl and beat together until light and fluffy. Gradually beat in the eggs and vanilla extract. Sift in the flour and baking powder and, using a metal spoon, fold in gently. Fold in the glacé cherries.

Spoon the mixture into the paper cases. Bake in the preheated oven for 25–30 minutes, until risen, golden and firm to the touch. Transfer to a wire rack and leave to cool.

To make the chocolate sauce, place the chocolate, butter and golden syrup in a heatproof bowl set over a saucepan of simmering water and leave until melted. Remove from the heat and stir until smooth. Leave to cool, stirring occasionally, for 20–30 minutes.

Whip the cream until holding firm peaks. Spoon into a piping bag fitted with a large star nozzle and pipe large swirls of cream on top of each cupcake. Drizzle over the chocolate sauce and sprinkle with the chopped nuts and pink sugar. Top each with a maraschino cherry.

Butterscotch Cupcakes

MAKES 28

175 g/6 oz plain flour

1 tbsp baking powder

175 g/6 oz butter, softened, or soft margarine

175 g/6 oz light muscovado sugar

3 eggs, lightly beaten

1 tsp vanilla extract

TOPPING

2 tbsp golden syrup

25 g/1 oz unsalted butter

2 tbsp light muscovado sugar

Preheat the oven to 190°C/375°F/Gas Mark 5. Put 28 paper cases into bun trays.

Sift the flour and baking powder into a large bowl. Add the butter, muscovado sugar, eggs and vanilla extract and, using an electric mixer, beat together until smooth.

Spoon the mixture into the paper cases. Bake in the preheated oven for 15–20 minutes, or until risen, golden and firm to the touch. Transfer to a wire rack and leave to cool.

To make the topping, place the golden syrup, butter and muscovado sugar in a small pan and heat gently, stirring, until the sugar dissolves. Bring to the boil and cook, stirring, for about 1 minute. Drizzle over the cupcakes and leave to set.

Coffee Fudge Cupcakes

MAKES 28

175 g/6 oz plain flour

1 tbsp baking powder

175 g/6 oz butter, softened, or soft margarine

175 g/6 oz caster sugar

3 eggs, lightly beaten

1 tsp coffee extract

2 tbsp milk

28 chocolate-covered coffee beans, to decorate

FROSTING

55 g/2 oz unsalted butter, softened

115 g/4 oz light muscovado sugar

2 tbsp single cream or milk

½ tsp coffee extract

400 g/14 oz icing sugar

Preheat the oven to 190°C/375°F/Gas Mark 5. Put 28 paper cases in bun trays.

Sift the flour and baking powder into a large bowl. Add the butter, caster sugar, eggs and coffee extract and, using an electric mixer, beat together until smooth. Beat in the milk.

Spoon the mixture into the paper cases. Bake in the preheated oven for 15–20 minutes, or until risen, golden and firm to the touch. Transfer the to a wire rack and leave to cool.

To make the frosting, place the butter, muscovado sugar, cream and coffee extract in a saucepan over a medium heat and stir until melted and smooth. Bring to the boil and boil, stirring, for 2 minutes. Remove from the heat and sift in the icing sugar. Stir the frosting until smooth and thick.

Spoon the frosting into a piping bag fitted with a large star nozzle. Pipe a swirl of frosting on top of each cupcake and top with a chocolate-covered coffee bean.

Pink Lemonade Cupcakes

MAKES 10

115 g/4 oz self-raising flour

¼ tsp baking powder

115 g/4 oz butter, softened, or soft margarine

115 g/4 oz caster sugar

2 large eggs, lightly beaten

pink food colouring

55 g/2 oz granulated sugar

juice of 1 small lemon

BUTTERCREAM

115 g/4 oz unsalted butter, softened

juice and finely grated rind of ½ lemon

4 tbsp double cream

225 g/8 oz icing sugar

pink food colouring

TO DECORATE

pink and white sugar sprinkles

pink, white and red hundreds and thousands

10 pink or yellow drinking straws

Preheat the oven to 180°C/350°F/Gas Mark 4. Put 10 paper cases in a bun tray.

Sift the flour and baking powder into a large bowl. Add the butter, caster sugar and eggs and, using an electric mixer, beat together until smooth. Beat in a little pink food colouring to colour the mixture pale pink.

Spoon the mixture into the paper cases. Bake in the preheated oven for 15–20 minutes, until risen and firm to the touch.

Meanwhile, place the granulated sugar and lemon juice in a small saucepan and heat gently, stirring, until the sugar has dissolved. Leave to cool for 15 minutes. Prick the tops of the warm cupcakes all over with a skewer and liberally brush with the lemon syrup. Transfer to a wire rack and leave to cool.

To make the buttercream, place the butter, lemon juice and lemon rind in a bowl and beat with an electric mixer for 2–3 minutes, until pale and creamy. Beat in the cream, then gradually sift in the icing sugar and continue beating for 2–3 minutes, until the buttercream is light and fluffy. Beat in a little pink food colouring to give a pale pink colour.

Using a small palette knife, thickly swirl the buttercream over the tops of the cupcakes. Scatter sugar sprinkles in the centre of 5 of cupcakes and edge the remaining cupcakes with hundreds and thousands. Cut the straws to 8-cm/3¼-inch lengths and push into the cupcakes.

Peaches & Cream Cupcakes

MAKES 12

400 g/14 oz canned peach slices in fruit juice

115 g/4 oz butter, softened, or soft margarine

115 g/4 oz caster sugar

2 eggs, lightly beaten

115 g/4 oz self-raising flour

150 ml/5 fl oz double cream

Preheat the oven to 180°C/350°F/Gas Mark 4. Put 12 paper cases in a muffin tray.

Drain the peaches, reserving the juice. Reserve 12 small slices and finely chop the remaining slices.

Place the butter and caster sugar in a large bowl and beat together until light and fluffy. Gradually beat in the eggs. Sift in the flour and, using a metal spoon, fold in gently. Fold in the chopped peaches and 1 tablespoon of the reserved juice.

Spoon the mixture into the paper cases. Bake in the preheated oven for 25 minutes, or until risen, golden and firm to the touch. Transfer to a wire rack and leave to cool.

Whip the cream until holding soft peaks. Using a small palette knife, spread the cream over the cupcakes. Top with the reserved peach slices.

Lemon Cheesecake Cupcakes

MAKES 12

60 g/2¼ oz butter, softened, or soft margarine

125 g/4½ oz digestive biscuits, crushed

85 g/3 oz caster sugar

275 g/9¾ oz full-fat cream cheese

2 large eggs, lightly beaten

finely grated rind of 1 large lemon

2 tsp lemon juice

125 ml/4 fl oz soured cream

35 g/1¼ oz plain flour

2 small lemons, thinly sliced, to decorate

Preheat the oven to 160°C/325°F/Gas Mark 3. Put 12 paper cases in a muffin tray.

Place the butter in a saucepan and heat gently until melted. Remove from the heat, then add the crushed biscuits and 1 tablespoon of the caster sugar and mix well. Spoon the biscuit mixture into the paper cases and press down firmly with the back of a teaspoon. Chill in the refrigerator.

Meanwhile, place the remaining caster sugar, the cream cheese and eggs in a large bowl and beat together until smooth. Add the lemon rind, lemon juice and soured cream and beat together until combined. Add the flour and beat well.

Spoon the cream cheese mixture into the paper cases. Bake in the preheated oven for 30 minutes, or until set but not browned. Transfer to a wire rack and leave to cool.

When the cupcakes are cold, chill in the refrigerator for at least 3 hours. Decorate each cupcake with a twisted lemon slice.

Neapolitan Cupcakes

MAKES 12

140 g/5 oz self-raising flour

½ tsp baking powder

140 g/5 oz butter, softened, or soft margarine

140 g/5 oz caster sugar

2 large eggs, lightly beaten

1 tsp vanilla extract

1 tbsp milk

1 tbsp cocoa powder mixed to a paste with 1½ tbsp hot water

FROSTING

175 g/6 oz full-fat cream cheese

115 g/4 oz unsalted butter, softened

350 g/12 oz icing sugar

1 tbsp strawberry jam, sieved

pink food colouring

TO DECORATE

chocolate strands

6 ice-cream wafers, each cut into 4 triangles

Preheat the oven to 180°C/350°F/Gas Mark 4. Put 12 paper cases in a muffin tray.

Sift the flour and baking powder into a large bowl. Add the butter, caster sugar and eggs and, using an electric mixer, beat together until smooth.

Divide the mixture between 2 bowls. Beat the vanilla extract and milk into 1 of the bowls and the cocoa powder paste into the other bowl.

Place alternate teaspoonfuls of the mixtures into the paper cases. Bake in the preheated oven for 15–20 minutes, until risen and firm to the touch. Transfer to a wire rack and leave to cool.

To make the frosting, put the cream cheese and butter in a bowl and blend together with a spatula. Sift in the icing sugar and beat until smooth and creamy. Divide the mixture between 2 bowls and stir the jam and a little pink food colouring into 1 of the bowls. Cover and chill both bowls of frosting in the refrigerator for 30 minutes.

Place alternate spoonfuls of the frostings into a large piping bag fitted with a large star nozzle. Pipe swirls of the frosting on the top of each cupcake. Sprinkle with chocolate strands and decorate each cupcake with 2 wafer triangles.

Sticky Date & Toffee Cupcakes

MAKES 6

85 g/3 oz dried stoned dates, chopped

½ tsp bicarbonate of soda

100 ml/3½ fl oz water

85 g/3 oz butter, softened, or soft margarine, plus extra for greasing

85 g/3 oz soft dark brown sugar

1 tsp vanilla extract

2 eggs, lightly beaten

115 g/4 oz self-raising flour

clotted cream, to serve

TOFFEE SAUCE

85 g/3 oz soft dark brown sugar

55 g/2 oz butter

4 tbsp double cream

Put the dates, bicarbonate of soda and water in a small saucepan and bring to the boil. Remove from the heat and set aside to cool.

Preheat the oven to 180°C/350°F/Gas Mark 4. Grease 6 x 150-ml/5-fl oz ovenproof teacups or ramekins.

Place the butter, brown sugar and vanilla extract in a large bowl and beat together until light and fluffy. Gradually beat in the eggs. Sift in the flour and, using a metal spoon, fold into the mixture followed by the date mixture.

Spoon the mixture into the teacups or ramekins. Put the teacups or ramekins on a baking sheet. Bake in the preheated oven for 20–25 minutes, or until risen and firm to the touch.

To make the toffee sauce, put all the ingredients in a small saucepan and heat until the butter has melted. Simmer for 5 minutes, stirring occasionally. Using a skewer, prick a few holes in each warm cupcake and drizzle over some of the sauce. Top with a little clotted cream and serve with the remaining toffee sauce.

Warm Molten-centred Chocolate Cupcakes

MAKES 8

85 g/3 oz self-raising flour

1 tbsp cocoa powder

55 g/2 oz butter, softened, or soft margarine

55 g/2 oz caster sugar

1 large egg, lightly beaten

55 g/2 oz plain chocolate

icing sugar, for dusting

Preheat the oven to 190°C/375°F/Gas Mark 5. Put 8 paper cases in a bun tray.

Sift the flour and cocoa powder into a large bowl. Add the butter, caster sugar and egg and, using an electric mixer, beat together until smooth.

Spoon half of the mixture into the paper cases. Using a teaspoon, make an indentation in the centre of each. Break the chocolate into 8 equal-sized squares and place a piece in each indentation, then spoon the remaining cake mixture on top.

Bake in the preheated oven for 20 minutes, or until risen and firm to the touch. Leave the cupcakes in the tin for 2–3 minutes before serving warm, dusted with icing sugar.

Tiramisu Cupcakes

MAKES 12

115 g/4 oz self-raising flour

½ tsp baking powder

115 g/4 oz butter, softened, or soft margarine

115 g/4 oz soft light brown sugar

2 eggs, lightly beaten

2 tbsp finely grated plain chocolate, to decorate

COFFEE SYRUP

2 tsp instant coffee granules

25 g/1 oz icing sugar

4 tbsp water

FROSTING

225 g/8 oz mascarpone cheese

85 g/3 oz caster sugar

2 tbsp Marsala or sweet sherry

Preheat the oven to 180°C/350°F/Gas Mark 4. Put 12 paper cases in a bun tray.

Sift the flour and baking powder into a large bowl. Add the butter, brown sugar and eggs and, using an electric mixer, beat together until smooth.

Spoon the mixture into the paper cases. Bake in the preheated oven for 15–20 minutes, or until risen, golden and firm to the touch.

Meanwhile, make the coffee syrup. Put the coffee granules, icing sugar and water in a pan and heat gently, stirring, until the coffee and sugar have dissolved. Boil for 1 minute, then leave to cool for 10 minutes.

Prick the tops of the warm cupcakes over all over with a skewer and brush with the coffee syrup. Transfer to a wire rack and leave to cool.

To make the frosting, put the mascarpone, caster sugar and Marsala in a bowl and beat together until smooth. Spread over the top of the cupcakes. Using a star stencil, sprinkle the grated chocolate over the frosting.

Ultimate Chocolate Cupcakes

MAKES 14

115 g/4 oz self-raising flour

½ tsp baking powder

1½ tbsp cocoa powder

115 g/4 oz butter, softened, or soft margarine

115 g/4 oz caster sugar

2 large eggs, lightly beaten

55 g/2 oz plain chocolate, melted

FROSTING

150 g/5½ oz plain chocolate, finely chopped

200 ml/7 fl oz double cream

140 g/5 oz unsalted butter, softened

280 g/10 oz icing sugar

TO DECORATE

piped chocolate shapes (see page 37)

gold dragées

Preheat the oven to 180°C/350°F/Gas Mark 4. Put 14 paper cases in bun trays.

Sift the flour, baking powder and cocoa powder into a large bowl. Add the butter, caster sugar and eggs and, using an electric mixer, beat together until smooth. Fold in the melted chocolate.

Spoon the mixture into the paper cases. Bake in the preheated oven for 15–20 minutes, or until risen and firm to the touch. Transfer to a wire rack and leave to cool.

To make the frosting, put the chocolate in a heatproof bowl. Heat the cream in a saucepan until boiling, then pour over the chocolate and stir until smooth. Leave to cool for 20 minutes, stirring occasionally, until thickened. Put the butter in a bowl, sift in the icing sugar and beat until smooth. Beat in the chocolate mixture. Chill for 15–20 minutes.

Spoon the frosting into a piping bag fitted with a large star nozzle. Pipe swirls of frosting on top of each cupcake. Decorate with piped chocolate shapes and gold dragées.

Chocolate Brownie Cupcakes

MAKES 12

225 g/8 oz plain chocolate, broken into pieces

85 g/3 oz butter, softened, or soft margarine

2 large eggs, lightly beaten

200 g/7 oz soft dark brown sugar

1 tsp vanilla extract

140 g/5 oz plain flour

75g/2¾ oz walnuts, chopped into small pieces

Preheat the oven to 180°C/350°F/Gas Mark 4. Put 12 paper cases in a muffin tray.

Place the chocolate and butter in a saucepan and heat gently, stirring constantly, until melted. Remove from the heat and stir until smooth. Leave to cool slightly.

Place the eggs and brown sugar in a large bowl and beat together, then add the vanilla extract. Sift in the flour and fold in gently, then stir in the melted chocolate mixture until combined. Stir in the chopped walnuts.

Spoon the mixture into the paper cases. Bake in the preheated oven for 30 minutes, or until firm to the touch but still slightly moist in the centre. Transfer to a wire rack and leave to cool.

Double Chocolate Cupcakes

MAKES 18

85 g/3 oz white chocolate, broken into pieces

1 tbsp milk

115 g/4 oz self-raising flour

½ tsp baking powder

115 g/4 oz butter, softened, or soft margarine

115 g/4 oz caster sugar

2 eggs, lightly beaten

1 tsp vanilla extract

TOPPING

140 g/5 oz milk chocolate, broken into pieces

18 white chocolate buttons

Preheat the oven to 190°C/375°F/Gas Mark 5. Put 18 paper cases in bun trays.

Place the white chocolate in a heatproof bowl and add the milk. Set the bowl over a saucepan of simmering water and heat until melted. Remove from the heat and stir gently until smooth.

Sift the flour and baking powder into a large bowl. Add the butter, caster sugar, eggs and vanilla extract and, using an electric mixer, beat together until smooth. Fold in the melted white chocolate mixture.

Spoon the mixture into the paper cases. Bake in the preheated oven for 20 minutes, or until risen, golden and firm to the touch. Transfer to a wire rack and leave to cool.

To make the topping, place the chocolate in a heatproof bowl and set the bowl over a saucepan of gently simmering water until melted. Leave to cool for 5 minutes, then spread over the tops of the cupcakes. Decorate each cupcake with a chocolate button.

Mocha Cupcakes

MAKES 20

2 tbsp instant espresso coffee powder

85 g/3 oz butter, softened, or soft margarine

85 g/3 oz caster sugar

1 tbsp honey

200 ml/7 fl oz water

225 g/8 oz plain flour

2 tbsp cocoa powder

1 tsp bicarbonate of soda

3 tbsp milk

1 large egg, lightly beaten

TOPPING

225 ml/8 fl oz whipping cream

cocoa powder, for dusting

Preheat the oven to 180°C/350°F/Gas Mark 4. Put 20 paper cases in bun trays.

Put the coffee powder, butter, caster sugar, honey and water in a saucepan and heat gently, stirring, until the sugar has dissolved. Bring to the boil, then reduce the heat and simmer for 5 minutes. Pour into a large heatproof bowl and leave to cool.

When the mixture has cooled, sift in the flour and cocoa powder. Dissolve the bicarbonate of soda in the milk, then add to the mixture with the egg and beat together until smooth.

Spoon the mixture into the paper cases. Bake in the preheated oven for 15–20 minutes, or until risen and firm to the touch. Transfer to a wire rack and leave to cool.

To make the topping, whisk the cream in a bowl until it hold its shape. Spoon a teaspoonful of cream on top of each cupcake, then dust with cocoa powder.

Chocolate & Hazelnut Cupcakes

MAKES 18

175 g/6 oz butter, softened, or soft margarine

115 g/4 oz soft light brown sugar

2 large eggs, lightly beaten

2 tbsp chocolate and hazelnut spread

175 g/6 oz self-raising flour

55 g/2 oz blanched hazelnuts, roughly ground

TOPPING

5 tbsp chocolate and hazelnut spread

18 whole blanched hazelnuts

Preheat the oven to 180°C/350°F/Gas Mark 4. Put 18 paper cases in bun trays.

Put the butter and brown sugar in a large bowl and beat together until light and fluffy. Gradually beat in the eggs, then stir in the chocolate and hazelnut spread. Sift in the flour and, using a metal spoon, fold into the mixture with the ground hazelnuts.

Spoon the mixture into the paper cases. Bake in the preheated oven for 20–25 minutes, or until risen and firm to the touch. Transfer to a wire rack and leave to cool.

Spread the chocolate and hazelnut spread over the cupcakes and top each with a blanched hazelnut.

Chocolate & Orange Cupcakes

MAKES 16

115 g/4 oz butter, softened, or soft margarine

115 g/4 oz caster sugar

finely grated rind and juice of ½ orange

2 eggs, lightly beaten

115 g/4 oz self-raising flour

25 g/1 oz plain chocolate, grated

thin strips of candied orange peel, to decorate

FROSTING

115 g/4 oz plain chocolate, broken into pieces

25 g/1 oz unsalted butter

1 tbsp golden syrup

Preheat the oven to 180°C/350°F/Gas Mark 4. Put 16 paper cases in bun trays.

Put the butter, caster sugar and orange rind in a large bowl and beat together until light and fluffy. Gradually beat in the eggs. Sift in the flour and, using a metal spoon, fold gently into the mixture with the orange juice and grated chocolate.

Spoon the mixture into the paper cases. Bake in the preheated oven for 20 minutes, or until risen, golden and firm to the touch. Transfer to a wire rack and leave to cool.

To make the frosting, place the chocolate in a heatproof bowl and add the butter and golden syrup. Set the bowl over a saucepan of simmering water and heat until melted. Remove from the heat and stir until smooth. Leave to cool until the frosting is thick enough to spread.

Spread the frosting over the cupcakes and decorate each with a few strips of candied orange peel. Leave to set.

Chocolate Cupcakes with Cream Cheese Frosting

MAKES 18

85 g/3 oz butter, softened, or soft margarine

100 g/3½ oz caster sugar

2 eggs, lightly beaten

225 g/8 oz self-raising flour

25 g/1 oz cocoa powder

2 tbsp milk

55 g/2 oz plain chocolate chips

chocolate curls, to decorate

FROSTING

225 g/8 oz white chocolate, broken into pieces

150 g/5½ oz low-fat cream cheese

Preheat the oven to 200°C/400°F/Gas Mark 6. Put 18 paper cases in bun trays.

Place the butter and caster sugar in a large bowl and beat together until light and fluffy. Gradually beat in the eggs. Sift in the flour and cocoa powder and, using a metal spoon, fold gently into the mixture with the milk and chocolate chips.

Spoon the mixture into the paper cases. Bake in the preheated oven for 20 minutes, or until risen and firm to the touch. Transfer to a wire rack and leave to cool.

To make the frosting, place the chocolate in a heatproof bowl and set the bowl over a saucepan of simmering water until melted. Leave to cool slightly. Put the cream cheese in a bowl and beat until softened, then beat in the melted chocolate.

Spread a little of the frosting over the top of each cupcake and decorate with chocolate curls. Leave to chill in the refrigerator for 1 hour before serving.

133

Pear & Chocolate Cupcakes

MAKES 12

100 g/3½ oz self-raising flour

½ tsp baking powder

2 tbsp cocoa powder

115 g/4 oz butter, softened, or soft margarine

115 g/4 oz soft light brown sugar

2 eggs, lightly beaten

4 canned pear halves, drained and sliced

2 tbsp honey, warmed

Preheat the oven to 190°C/375°F/Gas Mark 5. Put 12 paper cases in a bun tray.

Sift the flour, baking powder and cocoa powder into a large bowl. Add the butter, brown sugar and eggs and, using an electric mixer, beat together until smooth.

Spoon the mixture into the paper cases. Arrange the pear slices on top of the cupcakes. Bake in the preheated oven for 20 minutes, or until risen and firm to the touch. Transfer to a wire rack and, while still warm, glaze with the honey. Leave to cool.

Chocolate Flake Cupcakes

MAKES 30

175 g/6 oz plain flour

1 tbsp baking powder

175 g/6 oz butter, softened, or soft margarine

175 g/6 oz caster sugar

3 eggs, lightly beaten

1 tsp vanilla extract

2 tbsp milk

1 tbsp cocoa powder

70 g/2½ oz chocolate flake bars, crumbled

3 tbsp apricot jam, warmed

Preheat the oven to 190°C/375°F/Gas Mark 5. Put 30 paper cases in bun trays.

Sift the flour and baking powder into a large bowl. Add the butter, caster sugar, eggs and vanilla extract and, using an electric mixer, beat together until smooth. Mix the milk with the cocoa powder and stir into the mixture.

Spoon the mixture into the paper cases and sprinkle with about a quarter of the crumbled chocolate. Bake in the preheated oven for 15–20 minutes, or until risen and firm to the touch. Transfer to a wire rack and leave to cool.

When the cupcakes are cold, brush the tops with the jam and sprinkle with the remaining crumbled chocolate.

Chocolate Paradise Cupcakes

MAKES 16

85 g/3 oz plain chocolate, broken into pieces

50 ml/2 fl oz milk

1 tbsp cocoa powder

115 g/4 oz butter, softened, or soft margarine

115 g/4 oz dark muscovado sugar

2 large eggs, lightly beaten

3 tbsp soured cream

175 g/6 oz plain flour

½ tsp bicarbonate of soda

TOPPING

115 g/4 oz white marshmallows

3 tbsp milk

300 ml/10 fl oz double cream

55 g/2 oz desiccated coconut

55 g/2 oz plain chocolate, melted

Preheat the oven to 180°C/350°F/Gas Mark 4. Put 16 paper cases in bun trays.

Place the chocolate, milk and cocoa powder in a heatproof bowl set over a saucepan of simmering water and leave until the chocolate has melted. Remove from the heat and stir until smooth.

Place the butter and muscovado sugar in a large bowl and beat together until light and fluffy. Gradually beat in the eggs, then beat in the melted chocolate mixture and soured cream. Sift in the flour and bicarbonate of soda and, using a metal spoon, fold in gently.

Spoon the mixture into the paper cases. Bake in the preheated oven for 18–20 minutes, or until risen and firm to the touch. Transfer to a wire rack and leave to cool.

Place the marshmallows and milk in a heatproof bowl set over a saucepan of simmering water. Leave until the marshmallows have melted, stirring occasionally. Remove from the heat and leave to cool. Whip the cream until holding firm peaks, then fold into the marshmallow mixture with 35 g/1¼ oz of the desiccated coconut. Cover and chill in the refrigerator for 30 minutes.

Spread the frosting on top of the cupcakes. Sprinkle over the remaining desiccated coconut. Spoon the melted chocolate into a small paper piping bag, snip off the end and pipe criss-cross lines over the top of each cupcake. Leave to set.

Chocolate Honeycomb Cupcakes

MAKES 30

175 g/6 oz plain flour

1 tbsp baking powder

175 g/6 oz butter, softened, or soft margarine

175 g/6 oz caster sugar

3 eggs, lightly beaten

1 tsp vanilla extract

85 g/3 oz chocolate-covered honeycomb, finely chopped

ICING

200 g/7 oz icing sugar

2 tsp cocoa powder

about 2 tbsp water

Preheat the oven to 190°C/375°F/Gas Mark 5. Put 30 paper cases in bun trays.

Sift the flour and baking powder into a large bowl. Add the butter, caster sugar, eggs and vanilla extract and, using an electric mixer, beat together until smooth. Stir in half of the honeycomb.

Spoon the mixture into the paper cases. Bake in the preheated oven for 15–20 minutes, or until risen, golden and firm to the touch. Transfer to a wire rack and leave to cool.

To make the icing, sift the icing sugar and cocoa powder into a bowl and stir in the water to make a smooth paste. Spoon the icing over the cupcakes and top with the remaining honeycomb. Leave to set.

Dark & Light Cupcakes

MAKES 20

200 ml/7 fl oz water

85 g/3 oz butter

85 g/3 oz caster sugar

1 tbsp golden syrup

3 tbsp milk

1 tsp vanilla extract

1 tsp bicarbonate of soda

225 g/8 oz plain flour

2 tbsp cocoa powder

plain and white chocolate shavings, to decorate

FROSTING

50 g/1¾ oz plain chocolate, broken into pieces

4 tbsp water

50 g/1¾ oz unsalted butter

50 g/1¾ oz white chocolate, broken into pieces

350 g/12 oz icing sugar

Preheat the oven to 180°C/350°F/Gas Mark 4. Put 20 paper cases in bun trays.

Place the water, butter, caster sugar and golden syrup in a saucepan and heat gently, stirring, until the sugar has dissolved. Bring to the boil, then reduce the heat and simmer gently for 5 minutes. Leave to cool.

Meanwhile, place the milk and vanilla extract in a small bowl. Add the bicarbonate of soda and stir to dissolve. Sift the flour and cocoa powder into a separate large bowl and add the syrup mixture. Stir in the milk mixture and beat until smooth.

Spoon the mixture into the paper cases. Bake in the preheated oven for 20 minutes, or until risen and firm to the touch. Transfer to a wire rack and leave to cool.

To make the frosting, place the plain chocolate in a small heatproof bowl with 2 tablespoons of the water and half of the butter. Set the bowl over a saucepan of gently simmering water and heat until melted. Stir until smooth and then leave to stand over the water. Repeat with the white chocolate and remaining water and butter. Sift 175 g/6 oz of the icing sugar into each bowl and beat until smooth and thick.

Top half of the cupcakes with the plain chocolate frosting and half with the white chocolate frosting. Decorate with chocolate shavings and leave to set.

Chocolate Chip Cupcakes

MAKES 12

100 g/3½ oz self-raising flour

100 g/3½ oz butter, softened, or soft margarine

100 g/3½ oz caster sugar

2 large eggs, lightly beaten

100 g/3½ oz plain chocolate chips

Preheat the oven to 190°C/375°F/Gas Mark 5. Put 12 paper cases in a bun tray.

Sift the flour into a large bowl. Add the butter, caster sugar and eggs and, using an electric mixer, beat together until smooth. Fold in the chocolate chips.

Spoon the mixture into the paper cases. Bake in the preheated oven for 20–25 minutes, or until risen, golden and firm to the touch. Transfer to a wire rack and leave to cool.

Devil's Food Cupcakes

MAKES 18

115 g/4 oz plain flour

½ tsp bicarbonate of soda

25 g/1 oz cocoa powder

50 g/1¾ oz butter, softened, or soft margarine

115 g/4 oz soft dark brown sugar

2 large eggs, lightly beaten

125 ml/4 fl oz soured cream

chocolate caraque, to decorate

FROSTING

125 g/4½ oz plain chocolate, broken into pieces

2 tbsp caster sugar

150 ml/5 fl oz soured cream

Preheat the oven to 180°C/350°F/Gas Mark 4. Put 18 paper cases in bun trays.

Sift the flour, bicarbonate of soda and cocoa powder into a large bowl. Add the butter, brown sugar and eggs and, using an electric mixer, beat together until smooth. Fold in the soured cream.

Spoon the mixture into the paper cases. Bake in the preheated oven for 20 minutes, or until risen and firm to the touch. Transfer to a wire rack and leave to cool.

To make the frosting, place the chocolate in a heatproof bowl. Set the bowl over a saucepan of gently simmering water and heat until melted, stirring occasionally. Remove from the heat and leave to cool slightly, then beat in the caster sugar and soured cream until combined.

Spread the frosting over the tops of the cupcakes and decorate with chocolate caraque. Leave to set.

Tiny Chocolate Cupcakes

MAKES 20

55 g/2 oz butter, softened, or soft margarine

55 g/2 oz caster sugar

1 large egg, lightly beaten

55 g/2 oz self-raising flour

2 tbsp cocoa powder

1 tbsp milk

20 chocolate-covered coffee beans, to decorate

FROSTING

100 g/3½ oz plain chocolate, broken into pieces

100 ml/3½ fl oz double cream

Preheat the oven to 190°C/375°F/Gas Mark 5. Put 20 paper cases in a mini muffin tray.

Place the butter and caster sugar in a large bowl and beat together until light and fluffy. Gradually beat in the egg. Sift in the flour and cocoa powder and, using a metal spoon, fold in gently. Stir in the milk.

Spoon the mixture into the paper cases. Bake in the preheated oven for 10–15 minutes, or until risen and firm to the touch. Transfer to a wire rack and leave to cool.

To make the frosting, place the chocolate in a saucepan and add the cream. Heat gently, stirring all the time, until the chocolate has melted. Pour into a large heatproof bowl and, using an electric mixer, beat the mixture for 10 minutes, or until thick, glossy and cool.

Spoon the frosting into a piping bag fitted with a large star nozzle. Pipe a swirl of frosting on top of each cupcake and decorate with a chocolate-covered coffee bean. Chill in the refrigerator for 1 hour before serving.

White Chocolate & Rose Cupcakes

MAKES 12

115 g/4 oz butter, softened, or soft margarine

115 g/4 oz caster sugar

1 tsp rose water

2 eggs, lightly beaten

115 g/4 oz self-raising flour

55 g/2 oz white chocolate, grated

sugar-frosted rose petals, to decorate (see page 42)

FROSTING

115 g/4 oz white chocolate, broken into pieces

2 tbsp milk

175 g/6 oz full-fat cream cheese

25 g/1 oz icing sugar

Preheat the oven to 180°C/350°F/Gas Mark 4. Put 12 paper cases in a bun tray.

Place the butter, caster sugar and rose water in a large bowl and beat together until light and fluffy. Gradually beat in the eggs. Sift in the flour and, using a metal spoon, fold in gently. Fold in the grated chocolate.

Spoon the mixture into the paper cases. Bake in the preheated oven for 15–20 minutes, or until risen, golden and firm to the touch. Transfer to a wire rack and leave to cool.

To make the frosting, place the chocolate and milk in a heatproof bowl set over a pan of simmering water and leave until melted. Remove from the heat and stir until smooth. Leave to cool for 30 minutes. Put the cream cheese in a separate bowl, sift in the icing sugar and beat together until smooth and creamy. Fold in the melted chocolate. Chill in the refrigerator for 1 hour.

Swirl the frosting over the top of the cupcakes. Decorate with sugar-frosted rose petals.

Fruit & Nut

Banana & Pecan Cupcakes

MAKES 24

115 g/4 oz butter,
softened, or soft
margarine

115 g/4 oz caster sugar

½ tsp vanilla extract

2 eggs, lightly beaten

2 ripe bananas, mashed

4 tbsp soured cream

225 g/8 oz plain flour

1¼ tsp baking powder

¼ tsp bicarbonate of soda

55 g/2 oz pecan nuts,
roughly chopped

24 pecan nut halves,
to decorate

BUTTERCREAM

115 g/4 oz unsalted
butter, softened

175 g/6 oz icing sugar

Preheat the oven to 190°C/375°F/Gas Mark 5. Put 24 paper cases in bun trays.

Place the butter, caster sugar and vanilla extract in a large bowl and beat together until light and fluffy. Gradually beat in the eggs. Stir in the mashed bananas and soured cream. Sift in the flour, baking powder and bicarbonate of soda and, using a metal spoon, fold into the mixture with the chopped pecan nuts.

Spoon the mixture into the paper cases. Bake in the preheated oven for 20 minutes, or until risen, golden and firm to the touch. Transfer to a wire rack and leave to cool.

To make the buttercream, put the butter in a bowl and beat until fluffy. Sift in the icing sugar and mix together well.

Spoon the buttercream into a large piping bag fitted with a large star nozzle. Pipe a swirl of buttercream on top of each cupcake and decorate with a pecan nut half.

Raspberry Almond Cupcakes

MAKES 14

115 g/4 oz butter, softened, or soft margarine

85 g/3 oz caster sugar

½ tsp almond extract

2 eggs, lightly beaten

85 g/3 oz self-raising flour

55 g/2 oz ground almonds

85 g/3 oz fresh raspberries

2 tbsp flaked almonds

icing sugar, for dusting

Preheat the oven to 180°C/350°F/Gas Mark 4. Put 14 paper cases in bun trays.

Place the butter, caster sugar and almond extract in a large bowl and beat together until light and fluffy. Gradually beat in the eggs. Sift in the flour and, using a metal spoon, fold into the mixture with the ground almonds. Gently fold in the raspberries.

Spoon the mixture into the paper cases. Scatter the flaked almonds over the top. Bake in the preheated oven for 25–30 minutes, or until risen, golden and firm to the touch. Transfer to a wire rack and leave to cool. Dust with icing sugar.

Blueberry Cupcakes with Soured Cream Frosting

MAKES 30

175 g/6 oz plain flour

1 tbsp baking powder

175 g/6 oz butter, softened, or soft margarine

175 g/6 oz caster sugar

3 eggs, lightly beaten

1 tsp vanilla extract

finely grated rind of ½ orange

150 g/5½ oz fresh blueberries

FROSTING

150 g/5½ oz icing sugar

3 tbsp soured cream

Preheat the oven to 190°C/375°F/Gas Mark 5. Put 30 paper cases into bun trays.

Sift the flour and baking powder into a large bowl. Add the butter, caster sugar, eggs and vanilla extract and, using an electric mixer, beat together until smooth. Stir in the orange rind and 100g/3½ oz of the blueberries.

Spoon the mixture into the paper cases. Bake in the preheated oven for 15–20 minutes, or until risen, golden and firm to the touch. Transfer to a wire rack and leave to cool.

To make the frosting, sift the icing sugar into a bowl and stir in the soured cream. Spoon a little of the frosting on top of each cupcake and decorate with the remaining blueberries. Leave to set.

Frosted Peanut Butter Cupcakes

MAKES 16

55 g/2 oz butter, softened, or soft margarine

225 g/8 oz soft light brown sugar

115 g/4 oz crunchy peanut butter

2 eggs, lightly beaten

1 tsp vanilla extract

225 g/8 oz plain flour

2 tsp baking powder

100 ml/3½ fl oz milk

chopped unsalted peanuts, to decorate

FROSTING

200 g/7 oz full-fat cream cheese

25 g/1 oz unsalted butter, softened

225 g/8 oz icing sugar

Preheat the oven to 180°C/350°F/Gas Mark 4. Put 16 paper cases in bun trays.

Place the butter, brown sugar and peanut butter in a large bowl and beat together for 1–2 minutes, or until well mixed. Gradually beat in the eggs, then add the vanilla extract. Sift in the flour and baking powder and, using a metal spoon, fold into the mixture with the milk.

Spoon the mixture into the paper cases. Bake in the preheated oven for 25 minutes, or until risen, golden and firm to the touch. Transfer to a wire rack and leave to cool.

To make the frosting, put the cream cheese and butter in a bowl and beat together until smooth. Sift the icing sugar into the mixture and mix well.

Spoon the frosting into a piping bag fitted with a large star nozzle. Pipe a swirl of frosting on top of each cupcake and decorate with the chopped peanuts.

Vanilla, Hazelnut & Yogurt Cupcakes

MAKES 26

175 g/6 oz plain flour

2 tsp cornflour

1 tbsp baking powder

175 g/6 oz natural yogurt

175 g/6 oz caster sugar

3 eggs, lightly beaten

1 tsp vanilla extract

40 g/1½ oz hazelnuts, finely chopped

roughly chopped hazelnuts, to decorate

ICING

100 g/3½ oz icing sugar

40 g/1½ oz natural yogurt

Preheat the oven to 190°C/375°F/Gas Mark 5. Put 26 paper cases in bun trays.

Sift the flour, cornflour and baking powder into a large bowl. Add the yogurt, caster sugar, eggs and vanilla extract and, using an electric mixer, beat together until smooth. Stir in the finely chopped hazelnuts.

Spoon the mixture into the paper cases. Bake in the preheated oven for 15–20 minutes, or until risen, golden and firm to the touch. Transfer to a wire rack and leave to cool.

To make the icing, sift the icing sugar into a bowl and stir in the yogurt. Drizzle over the cupcakes and sprinkle with roughly chopped hazelnuts. Leave to set.

Mango & Passion Fruit Cupcakes

MAKES 18

115 g/4 oz butter, softened, or soft margarine

115 g/4 oz caster sugar

1 tsp finely grated orange rind

2 eggs, lightly beaten

115 g/4 oz self-raising flour

55 g/2 oz dried mango, finely chopped

1 tbsp orange juice

ICING

200 g/7 oz icing sugar

seeds and pulp from 1 passion fruit

1–2 tbsp orange juice

Preheat the oven to 190°C/375°F/Gas Mark 5. Put 18 paper cases in bun trays.

Place the butter, caster sugar and orange rind in a large bowl and beat together until light and fluffy. Gradually beat in the eggs. Sift in the flour and, using a metal spoon, fold into the mixture with the mango and orange juice.

Spoon the mixture into the paper cases. Bake in the preheated oven for 20 minutes, or until risen, golden and firm to the touch. Transfer to a wire rack and leave to cool.

To make the icing, sift the icing sugar into a bowl and add the passion fruit seeds and pulp and 1 tablespoon of the orange juice. Mix to a smooth icing, adding more orange juice if necessary. Spoon the icing over the cupcakes. Leave to set.

Hummingbird Cupcakes

MAKES 12

150 g/5½ oz plain flour

¾ tsp bicarbonate of soda

1 tsp ground cinnamon

125 g/4½ oz soft light brown sugar

2 eggs, lightly beaten

100 ml/3½ fl oz sunflower oil

1 ripe banana, mashed

2 canned pineapple rings, drained and finely chopped

25 g/1 oz pecan nuts, finely chopped

12 pecan nut pieces, to decorate

FROSTING

140 g/5 oz full-fat cream cheese

70 g/2½ oz unsalted butter, softened

1 tsp vanilla extract

280 g/10 oz icing sugar

Preheat the oven to 180°C/350°F/Gas Mark 4. Put 12 paper cases in a bun tray.

Sift the flour, bicarbonate of soda and cinnamon into a bowl and stir in the brown sugar. Add the eggs, oil, banana, pineapple and chopped pecan nuts and mix thoroughly.

Spoon the mixture into the paper cases. Bake in the preheated oven for 15–20 minutes, or until risen, golden and firm to the touch. Transfer to a wire rack and leave to cool.

To make the frosting, put the cream cheese, butter and vanilla extract in a bowl and blend together with a spatula. Sift in the icing sugar and beat until smooth and creamy.

Spoon the frosting into a piping bag fitted with a large star nozzle. Pipe a wavy line of frosting on top of each cupcake and decorate with pecan nut pieces.

Carrot Cake Cupcakes

MAKES 12

175 g/6 oz butter, softened, or soft margarine

115 g/4 oz caster sugar

2 eggs, lightly beaten

300 g/10½ oz carrots, grated

55 g/2 oz walnuts, finely chopped

2 tbsp orange juice

grated rind of ½ orange

175 g/6 oz self-raising flour

1 tsp ground cinnamon

12 walnut halves, to decorate

FROSTING

115 g/4 oz full-fat cream cheese

1 tbsp orange juice

225 g/8 oz icing sugar

Preheat the oven to 180°C/350°F/Gas Mark 4. Put 12 paper cases a muffin tray.

Place the butter and caster sugar in a large bowl and beat together until light and fluffy. Gradually beat in the eggs. Fold in the carrots, chopped walnuts, orange juice and orange rind. Sift in the flour and cinnamon and, using a metal spoon, fold in gently.

Spoon the mixture into the paper cases. Bake in the preheated oven for 15–20 minutes, or until risen, golden and firm to the touch. Transfer to a wire rack and leave to cool.

To make the frosting, put the cream cheese and orange juice in a bowl. Sift in the icing sugar and beat until fluffy. Spread the frosting over the cupcakes and top each with a walnut half.

Macadamia & Maple Cupcakes

MAKES 10

85 g/3 oz butter, softened, or soft margarine

55 g/2 oz soft light brown sugar

2 tbsp maple syrup

1 large egg, lightly beaten

85 g/3 oz self-raising flour

55 g/2 oz macadamia nuts, chopped

1 tbsp milk

2 tbsp lightly toasted chopped macadamia nuts, to decorate

FROSTING

25 g/1 oz unsalted butter, softened

2 tbsp maple syrup

85 g/3 oz icing sugar

85 g/3 oz cream cheese

Preheat the oven to 190°C/375°F/Gas Mark 5. Put 10 paper cases in a bun tray.

Place the butter, brown sugar and maple syrup in a large bowl and beat together until light and fluffy. Gradually beat in the egg. Sift in the flour and, using a metal spoon, fold into the mixture with the nuts and milk.

Spoon the mixture into the paper cases. Bake in the preheated oven for 20 minutes, or until risen, golden and firm to the touch. Transfer to a wire rack and leave to cool.

To make the frosting, beat the butter and maple syrup together until smooth. Sift in the icing sugar and beat in thoroughly. Gently beat in the cream cheese. Swirl the frosting on top of the cupcakes and decorate with the toasted nuts.

Apple Streusel Cupcakes

MAKES 14

½ tsp bicarbonate of soda

280 g/10 oz apple sauce (from a jar)

55 g/2 oz butter, softened, or soft margarine

85 g/3 oz demerara sugar

1 large egg, lightly beaten

175 g/6 oz self-raising flour

½ tsp ground cinnamon

½ tsp freshly grated nutmeg

TOPPING

50 g/1¾ oz plain flour

50 g/1¾ oz demerara sugar

¼ tsp ground cinnamon

¼ tsp freshly grated nutmeg

35 g/1¼ oz butter

Preheat the oven to 180°C/350°F/Gas Mark 4. Put 14 paper cases in bun trays.

To make the topping, put the flour, demerara sugar, cinnamon and nutmeg in a bowl. Cut the butter into small pieces, then add to the bowl and rub it in with your fingertips until the mixture resembles fine breadcrumbs.

Add the bicarbonate of soda to the apple sauce and stir until dissolved. Place the butter and demerara sugar in a large bowl and beat together until light and fluffy. Gradually beat in the egg. Sift in the flour, cinnamon and nutmeg and, using a metal spoon, fold into the mixture, alternating with the apple sauce.

Spoon the mixture into the paper cases. Scatter the topping over the cupcakes and press down gently. Bake in the preheated oven for 20 minutes, or until risen, golden and firm to the touch. Transfer to a wire rack and leave to cool.

Pistachio Cupcakes

MAKES 16

85 g/3 oz unsalted pistachio nuts

115 g/4 oz butter, softened, or soft margarine

140 g/5 oz caster sugar

140 g/5 oz self-raising flour

2 eggs, lightly beaten

4 tbsp Greek-style yogurt

1 tbsp chopped pistachio nuts, to decorate

BUTTERCREAM

115 g/4 oz unsalted butter, softened

2 tbsp lime juice cordial

green food colouring (optional)

200 g/7 oz icing sugar

Preheat the oven to 180°C/350°F/Gas Mark 4. Put 16 paper cases in bun trays.

Put the pistachio nuts in a food processor or blender and process for a few seconds until finely ground. Add the butter, caster sugar, flour, eggs and yogurt and then process until evenly mixed.

Spoon the mixture into the paper cases. Bake in the preheated oven for 20–25 minutes, or until risen, golden and firm to the touch. Transfer to a wire rack and leave to cool.

To make the buttercream, put the butter, lime cordial and a little green food colouring, if using, in a bowl and beat until fluffy. Sift in the icing sugar and beat until smooth. Swirl the buttercream over the cupcakes and decorate with the chopped pistachio nuts.

Pure Indulgence Almond Cupcakes

MAKES 12

100 g/3½ oz butter, softened, or soft margarine

100 g/3½ oz caster sugar

2 eggs, lightly beaten

¼ tsp almond extract

4 tbsp single cream

175 g/6 oz plain flour

1½ tsp baking powder

70 g/2½ oz ground almonds

toasted flaked almonds, to decorate

BUTTERCREAM

115 g/4 oz unsalted butter, softened

225 g/8 oz icing sugar

a few drops of almond extract

Preheat the oven to 180°C/350°F/Gas Mark 4. Put 12 paper cases a muffin tray.

Place the butter and caster sugar in a large bowl and beat together until light and fluffy. Gradually beat in the eggs, then add the almond extract and cream. Sift in the flour and baking powder and, using a metal spoon, fold into the mixture with the ground almonds.

Spoon the mixture into the paper cases. Bake in the preheated oven for 25 minutes, or until risen, golden and firm to the touch. Transfer to a wire rack and leave to cool.

To make the buttercream, place the butter in a large bowl and beat until creamy. Sift in the icing sugar, add the almond extract and beat together until smooth. Spread the buttercream over the cupcakes and decorate with flaked almonds.

Tropical Pineapple Cupcakes

MAKES 12

2 canned pineapple rings

85 g/3 oz butter, softened, or soft margarine

85 g/3 oz caster sugar

1 large egg, lightly beaten

85 g/3 oz self-raising flour

FROSTING

25 g/1 oz unsalted butter, softened

100 g/3½ oz cream cheese

grated rind of 1 lemon or lime

100 g/3½ oz icing sugar

about 1 tsp lemon juice or lime juice

Preheat the oven to 180°C/350°F/Gas Mark 4. Put 12 paper cases in a bun tray.

Drain the pineapple, reserving 1 tablespoon of the juice. Finely chop the pineapple. Place the butter and caster sugar in a large bowl and beat together until light and fluffy. Gradually beat in the egg. Sift in the flour and, using a large metal spoon, fold into the mixture. Fold in the chopped pineapple and the reserved pineapple juice.

Spoon the mixture into the paper cases. Bake in the preheated oven for 20 minutes, or until risen, golden and firm to the touch. Transfer to a wire rack and leave to cool.

To make the frosting, put the butter and cream cheese in a bowl and beat together until smooth. Add the lemon rind. Sift the icing sugar into the mixture, then beat together until well mixed. Gradually beat in the lemon juice, adding enough to form a spreading consistency.

Spoon the frosting into a piping bag fitted with a large star nozzle. Pipe a swirl of frosting on top of each cupcake.

Maple Pecan Cupcakes

MAKES 30

175 g/6 oz plain flour

1 tbsp baking powder

175 g/6 oz butter, softened, or soft margarine

115 g/4 oz light muscovado sugar

4 tbsp maple syrup

3 eggs, lightly beaten

1 tsp vanilla extract

30 g/1 oz pecan nuts, finely chopped

TOPPING

40 g/1½ oz pecan nuts, finely chopped

2 tbsp plain flour

2 tbsp light muscovado sugar

2 tbsp melted butter

Preheat the oven to 190°C/375°F/Gas Mark 5. Put 30 paper cases in bun trays.

Sift the flour and baking powder into a large bowl. Add the butter, muscovado sugar, maple syrup, eggs and vanilla extract and, using an electric mixer, beat together until smooth. Stir in the pecan nuts.

Spoon the mixture into the paper cases. To make the topping, mix together the pecan nuts, flour, muscovado sugar and melted butter to make a crumbly mixture and spoon a little on top of each cupcake.

Bake in the preheated oven for 15–20 minutes, or until risen, golden and firm to the touch. Transfer to a wire rack and leave to cool.

Lemon Polenta Cupcakes

MAKES 14

115 g/4 oz butter, softened, or soft margarine

115 g/4 oz golden caster sugar

finely grated rind and juice of ½ lemon

2 eggs, lightly beaten

55 g/2 oz plain flour

1 tsp baking powder

55 g/2 oz quick-cook polenta

14 crystallized violets, to decorate

FROSTING

150 g/5½ oz mascarpone cheese

25 g/1 oz icing sugar

2 tsp finely grated lemon rind

Preheat the oven to 180°C/350°F/Gas Mark 4. Put 14 paper cases in bun trays.

Place the butter and caster sugar in a large bowl and beat together until light and fluffy. Beat in the lemon rind and juice. Gradually beat in the eggs. Sift in the flour and baking powder and, using a metal spoon, fold gently into the mixture with the polenta.

Spoon the mixture into the paper cases. Bake in the preheated oven for 20 minutes, or until risen, golden and firm to the touch. Transfer to a wire rack and leave to cool.

To make the frosting, beat the mascarpone until smooth. Sift in the icing sugar, add the lemon rind and beat together until well mixed. Spread the frosting over the cupcakes and decorate with crystallized violets.

Shredded Orange Cupcakes

MAKES 12

85 g/3 oz butter, softened, or soft margarine

85 g/3 oz caster sugar

1 large egg, lightly beaten

85 g/3 oz self-raising flour

25 g/1 oz ground almonds

juice and grated rind of 1 small orange

15 g/½ oz toasted flaked almonds, to decorate

ORANGE SYRUP

juice and grated rind of 1 small orange

55 g/2 oz caster sugar

Preheat the oven to 180°C/350°F/Gas Mark 4. Put 12 paper cases in a bun tray.

Place the butter and caster sugar in a bowl and beat together until light and fluffy. Gradually beat in the egg. Sift in the flour and, using a large metal spoon, fold into the mixture with the ground almonds. Fold in the orange juice and rind.

Spoon the mixture into the paper cases. Bake in the preheated oven for 20–25 minutes, or until risen, golden and firm to the touch.

Meanwhile, make the orange syrup. Put the orange juice, orange rind and caster sugar in a saucepan and heat gently, stirring, until the sugar has dissolved, then simmer for 5 minutes.

Prick the tops of the warm cupcakes over all over with a skewer and spoon over the orange syrup. Scatter the flaked almonds on top. Transfer to a wire rack and leave to cool.

I ♥ You Cupcakes

MAKES 10

115 g/4 oz butter, softened, or soft margarine

115 g/4 oz caster sugar

1 tsp almond extract

2 large eggs, lightly beaten

115 g/4 oz self-raising flour

25 g/1 oz ground almonds

2 tbsp milk

3 tbsp raspberry jam

TO DECORATE

75 g/2¾ oz red ready-to-roll fondant icing

150 g/5½ oz white ready-to-roll fondant icing

1 tbsp egg white, lightly beaten

85 g/3 oz icing sugar, sifted, plus extra for dusting

Preheat the oven to 180°C/350°F/Gas Mark 4. Put 10 paper cases in a muffin tray.

Place the butter, caster sugar and almond extract in a large bowl and beat together until light and fluffy. Gradually beat in the eggs. Sift in the flour and, using a metal spoon, fold in gently with the ground almonds. Add the milk and fold gently into the mixture.

Spoon the mixture into the paper cases. Bake in the preheated oven for 20–25 minutes, until risen, golden and firm to the touch. Transfer to a wire rack and leave to cool.

Using a small knife, scoop a little of the sponge out from each cake. Place ½ teaspoon of the jam into each hollow and replace the piece of sponge on top.

Roll out a small piece of the red fondant icing and, using a small heart cutter, stamp out 2 hearts. Lightly knead the remaining red fondant icing into the white fondant icing to create a marbled effect. Roll out to a thickness of 5 mm/¼ inch on a surface lightly dusted with icing sugar. Use a 7-cm/2¾-inch cutter to stamp out 10 rounds. Brush the top of the cupcakes with the remaining jam and place the icing rounds on top.

Place the egg white in a bowl and gradually beat in the icing sugar to make a smooth icing. Spoon the icing into a small piping bag fitted with a fine writing nozzle. Pipe each of the letters I, Y, O and U on 2 cupcakes and attach the fondant hearts with a dab of water to the 2 remaining cupcakes.

Valentine Heart Cupcakes

MAKES 6

85 g/3 oz butter, softened, or soft margarine

85 g/3 oz caster sugar

½ tsp vanilla extract

2 eggs, lightly beaten

70 g/2½ oz plain flour

1 tbsp cocoa powder

1 tsp baking powder

6 sugar flowers, to decorate

MARZIPAN HEARTS

35 g/1¼ oz marzipan

red food colouring

icing sugar, for dusting

FROSTING

55 g/2 oz unsalted butter, softened

115 g/4 oz icing sugar

25 g/1 oz plain chocolate, melted

To make the marzipan hearts, knead the marzipan until pliable, then add a little red food colouring and knead until evenly coloured. Roll out the marzipan to a thickness of 5 mm/¼ inch on a surface lightly dusted with icing sugar. Using a small heart cutter, cut out 6 hearts. Place on a sheet of greaseproof paper dusted with icing sugar and leave to dry for 3–4 hours.

Preheat the oven to 180°C/350°F/Gas Mark 4. Put 6 paper cases in a muffin tray.

Place the butter, caster sugar and vanilla extract in a large bowl and beat together until light and fluffy. Gradually beat in the eggs. Sift in the flour, cocoa powder and baking powder and, using a metal spoon, fold into the mixture.

Spoon the mixture into the paper cases. Bake in the preheated oven for 20–25 minutes, or until risen and firm to the touch. Transfer to a wire rack and leave to cool.

To make the frosting, put the butter in a large bowl and beat until fluffy. Sift in the icing sugar and beat together until smooth. Add the melted chocolate and beat together until well mixed. Spread some of the frosting on top of each cupcake and decorate with a marzipan heart and sugar flower.

Rose Petal Cupcakes

MAKES 12

115 g/4 oz butter, softened, or soft margarine

115 g/4 oz caster sugar

2 eggs, lightly beaten

175 g/6 oz self-raising flour

1 tbsp milk

a few drops of rose oil essence

¼ tsp vanilla extract

sugar-frosted rose petals, to decorate (see page 42)

BUTTERCREAM

85 g/3 oz unsalted butter, softened

175 g/6 oz icing sugar

pink food colouring (optional)

Preheat the oven to 200°C/400°F/Gas Mark 6. Put 12 paper cases in a bun tray.

Place the butter and caster sugar in a large bowl and beat together until light and fluffy. Gradually beat in the eggs. Sift in the flour and, using a metal spoon, fold in gently. Stir in the milk, rose oil essence and vanilla extract.

Spoon the mixture into the paper cases. Bake in the preheated oven for 12–15 minutes, until risen, golden and firm to the touch. Transfer to a wire rack and leave to cool.

To make the buttercream, put the butter in a large bowl and beat until fluffy. Sift in the icing sugar and mix well together. Add a little pink food colouring, if using, to give a pale pink colour.

Spoon the buttercream into a piping bag fitted with a large plain nozzle. Pipe a blob of buttercream on top of each cupcake and decorate with sugar-frosted rose petals.

Wedding Cupcakes

MAKES 30

350 g/12 oz self-raising flour

1 tsp baking powder

225 g/8 oz butter, softened, or soft margarine

225 g/8 oz caster sugar

finely grated rind of 1 large lemon

4 large eggs, lightly beaten

2 tbsp milk

TO DECORATE

650 g/1 lb 7 oz white ready-to-roll fondant icing

3 tbsp apricot jam, warmed and sieved

15 white fondant roses, dipped in edible silver glitter (see page 40)

2 tbsp egg white, lightly beaten

150 g/5½ oz icing sugar, sifted, plus extra for dusting

Preheat the oven to 160°C/325°F/Gas Mark 3. Put 30 paper cases in bun trays.

Sift the flour and baking powder into a large bowl. Add the butter, caster sugar, lemon rind, eggs and milk and, using an electric mixer, beat together until smooth.

Spoon the mixture into the paper cases. Bake in the preheated oven for 20–25 minutes, until risen, golden and firm to the touch. Transfer to a wire rack and leave to cool.

Roll out the white fondant icing to a thickness of 5 mm/¼ inch on a surface lightly dusted with icing sugar. Using a 6-cm/2½-inch cutter, stamp out 30 rounds, re-rolling the icing as necessary. Brush each cupcake lightly with a little of the jam and gently press an icing round on top. Gently press a fondant rose into the centre of half the iced cupcakes.

Place the egg white in a bowl and gradually beat in the icing sugar to make a smooth icing. Spoon the icing into a small piping bag fitted with a fine writing nozzle. Starting at an edge, pipe a random meandering line of icing all over the surface of each plain cupcake. Try not to let the lines touch or cross and keep an even pressure on the piping bag so that the lines are of the same thickness. Leave to set.

Silver or Golden Anniversary Cupcakes

MAKES 24

225 g/8 oz butter, softened, or soft margarine

225 g/8 oz caster sugar

4 large eggs, lightly beaten

1 tsp vanilla extract

225 g/8 oz self-raising flour

5 tbsp milk

silver or gold dragées, to decorate

BUTTERCREAM

175 g/6 oz unsalted butter, softened

350 g/12 oz icing sugar

Preheat the oven to 180°C/350°F/Gas Mark 4. Put 24 silver or gold foil cases in bun trays.

Place the butter and caster sugar in a large bowl and beat together until light and fluffy. Gradually beat in the eggs and vanilla extract. Sift in the flour and, using a large metal spoon, fold into the mixture with the milk.

Spoon the mixture into the foil cases. Bake in the preheated oven for 15–20 minutes, or until risen, golden and firm to the touch. Transfer to a wire rack and leave to cool.

To make the buttercream, put the butter in a bowl and beat until fluffy. Sift in the icing sugar and beat together until smooth.

Spoon the buttercream into a piping bag fitted with a star nozzle. Pipe swirls of buttercream on top of each cupcake and decorate with silver or gold dragées.

Birthday Party Cupcakes

MAKES 24

225 g/8 oz self-raising flour

225 g/8 oz butter, softened, or soft margarine

225 g/8 oz caster sugar

4 eggs, lightly beaten

BUTTERCREAM

175 g/6 oz unsalted butter, softened

350 g/12 oz icing sugar

TO DECORATE

sugar sprinkles and sugar flowers

candles and candle holders (optional)

Preheat the oven to 180°C/350°F/Gas Mark 4. Put 24 paper cases in bun trays.

Sift the flour into a large bowl. Add the butter, caster sugar and eggs and, using an electric mixer, beat together until smooth.

Spoon the mixture into the paper cases. Bake in the preheated oven for 15–20 minutes, or until risen, golden and firm to the touch. Transfer to a wire rack and leave to cool.

To make the buttercream, put the butter in a bowl and beat until fluffy. Sift in the icing sugar and beat together until smooth and creamy.

Spoon the buttercream into a piping bag fitted with a large star nozzle. Pipe swirls of buttercream on top of each cupcake and decorate with sugar sprinkles and sugar flowers. If using, place a candle in the top of each.

New Baby Cupcakes

MAKES 12

115 g/4 oz self-raising flour

¼ tsp baking powder

115 g/4 oz butter, softened, or soft margarine

115 g/4 oz caster sugar

2 eggs, lightly beaten

1 tbsp milk

1 tsp vanilla extract

TO DECORATE

150 g/5½ oz white ready-to-roll fondant icing

icing sugar, for dusting

150 g/5½ oz pale blue or pink ready-to-roll fondant icing

1 tbsp apricot jam, warmed and sieved

tube of white writing icing

Preheat the oven to 180°C/350°F/Gas Mark 4. Put 12 paper cases in a bun tray.

Sift the flour and baking powder into a large bowl. Add the butter, caster sugar, eggs, milk and vanilla extract and, using an electric mixer, beat together until smooth.

Spoon the mixture into the paper cases. Bake in the preheated oven for 15–20 minutes, until risen, golden and firm to the touch. Transfer to a wire rack and leave to cool.

Roll out the white fondant icing to a thickness of 5 mm/¼ inch on a surface lightly dusted with icing sugar. Using a 6-cm/2½-inch cutter, stamp out 6 rounds. Repeat with the blue or pink fondant icing. Brush each cupcake lightly with a little of the jam and gently press an icing round on top.

Re-roll the blue or pink fondant icing trimmings. Use a small teddy bear cutter to stamp out 2 teddy bears. Use a tiny flower cutter to stamp out 4 flowers. Re-roll the white fondant icing trimmings. Use a small flower cutter to stamp out 2 small flowers. Use a 4-cm/1½-inch fluted cutter to stamp out 2 rounds, then cut away a small oval from each round to resemble a baby's bib. Use a 2.5-cm/1-inch cutter to stamp out 2 rounds and mark with the end of a paintbrush to resemble buttons. Shape 4 booties and 2 ducks from the remaining fondant icing trimmings.

Attach all the decorations to the top of the cupcakes with a little water. Use the writing icing to add the finishing touches, such as bows on the booties.

Easter Cupcakes

MAKES 12

115 g/4 oz butter, softened, or soft margarine

115 g/4 oz caster sugar

2 eggs, lightly beaten

85 g/3 oz self-raising flour

25 g/1 oz cocoa powder

36 mini candy-covered chocolate eggs, to decorate

BUTTERCREAM

85 g/3 oz unsalted butter, softened

175 g/6 oz icing sugar

1 tbsp milk

a few drops of vanilla extract

Preheat the oven to 180°C/350°F/Gas Mark 4. Put 12 paper cases in a bun tray.

Place the butter and caster sugar in a large bowl and beat together until light and fluffy. Gradually beat in the eggs. Sift in the flour and cocoa powder and, using a metal spoon, fold into the mixture.

Spoon the mixture into the paper cases. Bake in the preheated oven for 15–20 minutes, or until risen and firm to the touch. Transfer to a wire rack and leave to cool.

To make the buttercream, put the butter in a bowl and beat until fluffy. Sift in the icing sugar and beat together until well mixed, adding the milk and vanilla extract.

Spoon the buttercream into a piping bag fitted with a large star nozzle. Pipe a circle of buttercream on top of each cupcake to form a nest. Place 3 candy-covered chocolate eggs in the centre of each nest to decorate.

Marzipan Flower Cupcakes

MAKES 12

115 g/4 oz self-raising flour

½ tsp baking powder

115 g/4 oz butter, softened, or soft margarine

115 g/4 oz caster sugar

2 eggs, lightly beaten

a few drops of almond extract

TO DECORATE

200 g/7 oz marzipan

icing sugar, for dusting

2 tbsp apricot jam, sieved

Preheat the oven to 180°C/350°F/Gas Mark 4. Put 12 paper cases in a bun tray.

Sift the flour and baking powder into a large bowl. Add the butter, caster sugar, eggs and almond extract and, using an electric mixer, beat together until smooth.

Spoon the mixture into the paper cases. Bake in the preheated oven for 20 minutes, or until risen, golden and firm to the touch. Transfer to a wire rack and leave to cool.

Roll out the marzipan on a surface lightly dusted with icing sugar. Using a 3-cm/1¼-inch cutter, stamp out 60 rounds, re-rolling the marzipan as necessary. Spread a little jam over the top of each cupcake. Pinch the marzipan circles at 1 side to create petal shapes and arrange 5 petals on top of each cupcake. Roll the remaining marzipan into 12 small balls for the flower centres and place in the middle of the cupcakes.

Sweetshop Cupcakes

MAKES 12

150 g/5½ oz butter, softened, or soft margarine

150 g/5½ oz caster sugar

3 eggs, lightly beaten

150 g/5½ oz self-raising flour

4 tsp strawberry-flavoured popping candy

sweets of your choice, to decorate

BUTTERCREAM

175 g/6 oz unsalted butter, softened

2 tbsp milk

350 g/12 oz icing sugar

pink and yellow food colourings

Preheat the oven to 180°C/350°F/Gas Mark 4. Put 12 paper cases in a bun tray.

Place the butter and caster sugar in a large bowl and beat together until light and fluffy. Gradually beat in the eggs. Sift in the flour and, using a metal spoon, fold in gently. Fold in half of the popping candy.

Spoon the mixture into the paper cases. Bake in the preheated oven for 18–22 minutes, until risen, golden and firm to the touch. Transfer to a wire rack and leave to cool.

To make the buttercream, place the butter in a bowl and beat with an electric mixer for 2–3 minutes, until pale and creamy. Beat in the milk, then gradually sift in the icing sugar and continue beating for 2–3 minutes, until the buttercream is light and fluffy. Divide the buttercream between 2 bowls and beat a little pink or yellow food colouring into each bowl.

Pipe or swirl the buttercream on top of the cupcakes and decorate with sweets. Sprinkle over the remaining popping candy just before serving.

Toffee Apple Cupcakes

MAKES 16

2 eating apples

1 tbsp lemon juice

250 g/9 oz plain flour

2 tsp baking powder

1½ tsp ground cinnamon

70 g/2½ oz light muscovado sugar

55 g/2 oz butter, melted, plus extra for greasing

100 ml/3½ fl oz milk

100 ml/3½ fl oz apple juice

1 egg, lightly beaten

TOFFEE SAUCE

2 tbsp double cream

40 g/1½ oz light muscovado sugar

15 g/½ oz butter

Preheat the oven to 200°C/400°F/Gas Mark 6. Grease 16 holes in 2 bun trays.

Roughly grate 1 of the apples. Cut the remaining apple into 5 mm/¼ inch thick slices and toss in the lemon juice. Sift the flour, baking powder and cinnamon into a large bowl, then stir in the muscovado sugar and grated apple.

Combine the melted butter with the milk, apple juice and egg. Stir the liquid ingredients into the dry ingredients, mixing lightly until just combined.

Spoon the mixture into the prepared bun tray and arrange 2 of the apple slices on top of each cupcake. Bake in the preheated oven for 15–20 minutes, or until risen, golden and firm to the touch. Transfer to a wire rack and leave to cool.

For the toffee sauce, place all the ingredients in a small pan and heat, stirring, until the sugar is dissolved. Increase the heat and boil rapidly for 2 minutes, or until slightly thickened and syrupy. Cool slightly, then drizzle over the cupcakes and leave to set.

Halloween Spider Cupcakes

MAKES 12

115 g/4 oz self-raising flour

115 g/4 oz butter, softened, or soft margarine

115 g/4 oz caster sugar

2 eggs, lightly beaten

TO DECORATE

200 g/7 oz orange ready-to-roll fondant icing

icing sugar, for dusting

55 g/2 oz black ready-to-roll fondant icing

tubes of black and yellow writing icing

Preheat the oven to 180°C/350°F/Gas Mark 4. Put 12 paper cases in a bun tray.

Sift the flour into a large bowl. Add the butter, caster sugar and eggs and, using an electric mixer, beat together until smooth.

Spoon the mixture into the paper cases. Bake in the preheated oven for 15–20 minutes, or until risen, golden and firm to the touch. Transfer to a wire rack and leave to cool.

Roll out the orange fondant icing to a thickness of 5 mm/¼ inch on a surface lightly dusted with icing sugar. Using a 5.5-cm/2¼-inch plain cutter, stamp out 12 rounds, re-rolling the icing as necessary. Place an icing round on top of each cupcake.

Roll out the black fondant icing to the same thickness. Using a 3-cm/1¼-inch plain cutter, cut out 12 rounds and place 1 on the centre of each cupcake. Using black writing icing, pipe 8 legs onto each spider and, using yellow writing icing, pipe 2 eyes and a mouth.

Ghostly Ghoul Cupcakes

MAKES 6

85 g/3 oz butter, softened, or soft margarine

85 g/3 oz dark muscovado sugar

1 tbsp black treacle

2 large eggs, lightly beaten

140 g/5 oz plain flour

2 tsp ground mixed spice

¾ tsp bicarbonate of soda

BUTTERCREAM

85 g/3 oz unsalted butter, softened

1 tbsp dulce de leche

175 g/6 oz icing sugar

TO DECORATE

350 g/12 oz white ready-to-roll fondant icing

icing sugar, for dusting

tube of black writing icing

Preheat the oven to 180°C/350°F/Gas Mark 4. Put 12 paper cases in a bun tray and 6 paper cases in a mini muffin tray.

Place the butter, muscovado sugar and treacle in a bowl and beat together until light and fluffy. Gradually beat in the eggs. Sift in the flour, mixed spice and bicarbonate of soda and, using a metal spoon, fold in gently.

Spoon the mixture into the paper cases. Bake the mini muffins in the preheated oven for 10–12 minutes and the cupcakes for 15–20 minutes, until risen and firm to the touch. Transfer to a wire rack and leave to cool.

To make the buttercream, place the butter and dulce de leche in a bowl and beat with an electric mixer for 2–3 minutes, until pale and creamy. Gradually sift in the icing sugar and beat until smooth.

To assemble, remove the paper cases from half of the cupcakes and all the mini muffins. Level the tops of all the cakes if necessary. Spread a layer of buttercream over the top of the remaining cupcakes. Top each with an upturned cupcake and an upturned mini muffin. Spread the buttercream all over the stacked cakes. Chill in the refrigerator for 30 minutes.

Take 50 g/1¾ oz of the white fondant icing and roll into 6 small balls. Place 1 on top of each of the stacked cakes. Divide the remaining fondant into 6 pieces and roll out each piece on a surface lightly dusted with icing sugar to a 14-cm/5½-inch round with a thickness of about 3 mm/⅛ inch. Drape over the cupcakes. Use the black writing icing to pipe ghost faces on each cupcake.

Festive Holly Cupcakes

MAKES 16

125 g/4½ oz butter, softened, or soft margarine

200 g/7 oz caster sugar

4 eggs, lightly beaten

a few drops of almond extract

150 g/5½ oz self-raising flour

175 g/6 oz ground almonds

TO DECORATE

450 g/1 lb white ready-to-roll fondant icing

icing sugar, for dusting

55 g/2 oz green ready-to-roll fondant icing

25 g/1 oz red ready-to-roll fondant icing

Preheat the oven to 180°C/350°F/Gas Mark 4. Put 16 paper cases in a muffin tray.

Place the butter and caster sugar in a large bowl and beat together until light and fluffy. Gradually beat in the eggs and almond extract. Sift in the flour and, using a metal spoon, fold into the mixture with the ground almonds.

Spoon the mixture into the paper cases. Bake in the preheated oven for 20 minutes, or until risen, golden and firm to the touch. Transfer to a wire rack and leave to cool.

Roll out the white fondant icing to a thickness of 5 mm/¼ inch on a surface lightly dusted with icing sugar. Using a 7-cm/2¾-inch plain cutter, stamp out 16 rounds, re-rolling the icing as necessary. Place an icing round on top of each cupcake.

Roll out the green fondant icing to the same thickness. Using a holly cutter, cut out 32 leaves, re-rolling the icing as necessary. Brush each leaf with a little water and place 2 leaves on top of each cupcake. Roll the red fondant icing to form 48 small berries and place on the leaves.

Christmas Star Cupcakes

MAKES 12

85 g/3 oz butter, softened, or soft margarine

85 g/3 oz soft light brown sugar

1 large egg, lightly beaten

85 g/3 oz self-raising flour

½ tsp ground cinnamon

1 tbsp milk

GOLD STARS

85 g/3 oz yellow ready-to-roll fondant icing

icing sugar, for dusting

edible gold glitter (optional)

ICING

85 g/3 oz icing sugar

2–3 tsp lemon juice

Preheat the oven to 180°C/350°F/Gas Mark 4. Put 12 paper cases in a bun tray.

Place the butter and brown sugar in a large bowl and beat together until light and fluffy. Gradually beat in the egg. Sift in the flour and cinnamon and, using a metal spoon, fold into the mixture with the milk.

Spoon the mixture into the paper cases. Bake in the preheated oven for 20 minutes, or until risen, golden and firm to the touch. Transfer to a wire rack and leave to cool.

To make the gold stars, roll out the yellow fondant icing to a thickness of 5 mm/¼ inch on a surface lightly dusted with icing sugar. Using a small star cutter, stamp out 12 stars. Brush each star with a little gold glitter, if using. Set aside on a sheet of baking paper.

To make the icing, sift the icing sugar into a bowl and stir in enough of the lemon juice to make a smooth, thick icing.

Spoon the icing over the cupcakes and top each with a gold star. Leave to set.

Snowman Cupcakes

MAKES 10

115 g/4 oz butter, softened, or soft margarine

115 g/4 oz caster sugar

2 large eggs, lightly beaten

115 g/4 oz self-raising flour

85 g/3 oz desiccated coconut

2 tbsp milk

BUTTERCREAM

55 g/2 oz unsalted butter, softened

2 tbsp double cream

115 g/4 oz icing sugar

TO DECORATE

55 g/2 oz black ready-to-roll fondant icing

icing sugar, for dusting

glacé cherries, angelica, chocolate chips and orange jelly diamonds

Preheat the oven to 180°C/350°F/Gas Mark 4. Put 10 paper cases in a bun tray.

Place the butter and caster sugar in a large bowl and beat together until light and fluffy. Gradually beat in the eggs. Sift in the flour and, using a metal spoon, fold in gently. Fold in 55 g/2 oz of the desiccated coconut and the milk.

Spoon the mixture into the paper cases. Bake in the preheated oven for 15–20 minutes, until risen, golden and firm to the touch. Transfer to a wire rack and leave to cool.

To make the buttercream, place the butter in a bowl and beat with an electric mixer for 2–3 minutes, until pale and creamy. Beat in the cream, then gradually sift in the icing sugar and continue beating for 2–3 minutes, until the buttercream is light and fluffy.

Spread the buttercream over the cupcakes, using a palette knife to smooth and shape it into a slight mound. Sprinkle over the remaining desiccated coconut.

Roll out the black fondant icing on surface lightly dusted with icing sugar and cut out 10 hat shapes. Decorate each hat with small pieces of glacé cherry and angelica to resemble holly leaves and berries. Place on the cupcakes. Gently press 2 chocolate chips, a piece of jelly diamond and a rolled strip of black fondant icing on top of each cupcake for the snowman's eyes, nose and mouth.

Index

Happy baking!